Beyond The Agency Box

The Phoneless, Meetingless Digital Marketing
Agency That Creates Lifetime Happy Clients
Without Facebook Ads, Webinars, Google, or SEO

Frankie Fihn

Copyright © 2020 by Beyond Agency Profits.
All rights reserved.

This book or any portion thereof may not be reproduced or used in any manner whatsoever without the express written permission of the publisher except for the use of brief quotations in a book review.

Printed in the United States of America

First Printing, 2020

ISBN 9798668731992

Independently Published
http://www.beyondagencyprofits.com

Acknowledgements

Firstly, thanks to Ilka Bee. Without your continued support, understanding, and love this book could not have been written. You are the perfect partner and the mother I always wanted for our two children.

To my two children Heidi and Zelda. Thank you for inspiring your daddy to be better every day. Our nature walks are still my favorite part of every day.

To Travis Sago for your unending insights and support. Your ideas and wisdom made this book what it is. Thank you for always guiding us to serve more people more deeply.

Contents

Chapter 1: Why? 5

Chapter 2: The 5 Stages Of Agency Growth ….....13

Chapter 3: Solving Your Sales Woes Once And For All ………………………………………………....21

Chapter 4: The Agency Model Reimagined ….....37

Chapter 5: Absolutely Rocking Your Client Results ……………………………………………………...53

Chapter 6: Being In 100% Control Of Your Client Relationships ……………………………………...73

Chapter 7: An Automated Sales Machine Without The Phone ……………………………………….87

Chapter 8: *Scratches Ears* Good Boy! Training Your Clients To Behave …....……………………..111

Chapter 9: How To Exceed Expectations And Deliver A Wow Client Experience ……………….125

Chapter 10: The Thirty Year Wealth Shortcut ……………………………………….145

Chapter 11: The Journey Of Purpose, Ayahuasca, And A Perfect Average Day ....…..…..161

Chapter 12: Building A Team of A+ Superstars Who Make You Look Like A God ………………….191

Chapter 13: Uncertainty, Coronavirus, & Depressed Economies ………………....……………..205

Chapter 14: Beginning With The End In Mind ..213

Chapter 1: Why?

You are about to discover a brand new kind of digital marketing agency. You will reimagine, reengineer, and revamp everything you have been told you "have to" do. This new type of agency doesn't require you to be on the phone all day. It doesn't require you to constantly check your email or have endless client meetings. In fact, it will actually empty your calendar as you earn 7 figures and beyond.

At the core of this book is one big idea. You deserve a life of freedom while your income continues to grow. You will create this new life while making a profound difference in your clients' lives in the simplest and easiest way possible.

This may sound simple and obvious, yet is it rarely done in practice. Very few people in our society create money and freedom *together*. As money goes up, time and freedom goes down.

There are hoards of very "successful" doctors and lawyers who missed their children growing up. Many have big bank accounts and failed marriages.

Of course, being a broke freelancer struggling to pay rent shouldn't be your goal either. You don't want all the time in the world with endless money stress.

This book will guide you to that sweet place where you become abundant in time and money together. You will experience what only true freedom can buy. There is a heavy emphasis on your quality of life.

There is something no one tells you about this business. Creating a highly successful digital marketing agency is actually one of the hardest businesses in the world to scale. If you're not careful, you can build yourself a high-paying prison. While it's a great way to get started with little capital, it's actually very hard to play in the big leagues. Your time and energy can bring you to a screeching halt very quickly. It's easy to become burnt out and overworked fast.

That's why this book was created. It will help you through the 100's of potential pitfalls that cost you in your time, energy, or money.

Why are you here now reading this book? Why did you want this life? Why did you choose this path? Why did you make the decisions you made?

Why did you decide to work for yourself? Of all the unlimited choices you had, why did you start a digital marketing agency?

Why didn't you just get a regular job like everybody else? Why didn't you take the easy way out?

Why did you put in time and effort learning these skills? Why do you want to share those skills with other deserving businesses? Why not just keep these secrets only to yourself? Why didn't you just push the next shady affiliate product onto the world?

I'm willing to bet that you had reasons. Damn good reasons. However, I bet the reality of things feels and looks *just* a bit different from your dream, doesn't it?

Does This Sound Like Your Agency?

Do you spend most of your days working isolated by yourself on a computer in a dark room? Or are you the only one you know working late on a Sunday night when everybody else is taking it easy?

Do you find yourself checking your email more than 20 times per day? Or do you feel constantly tethered to your phone like it's an electronic leash? Or is your calendar fully booked some days? Or do you spend the last moments on your pillow at night worried about how you will get results for your clients?

Do you sometimes feel like "working for yourself" means you have a hundred different bosses? Or do you end up in client-underlying relationships where you are the underling? Does more clients mean more "have tos"?

Do you feel the pinch of rising ad costs? Or do you worry about the next ad account being shut down? Or do you worry about the next Google update?

Do you find yourself having to make yet another sales call? Or do you have to write another proposal to a potential client only to have them disappear later? Or do you chase potential clients asking if they read your proposal yet? Or do they ghost you without just being honest about "I'm in" or "I'm out"?

Do you ever lose a job to a competitor who you know is going to deliver crap results? Or do they go with someone else just because "they were cheaper"?

Do you have constant meeting requests from the clients you already have? Or do they ask you to explain the same thing that you've already explained 100 times? Or do you ever have a client who speaks to you in a condescending tone? Or do you retain most clients for 12 months or less even if you're doing a good job?

Do you find yourself drowning in another Wordpress error that you've tried to Google the answer for 3 hours? Or do you stare at a screen trying to find an unknown error in 100 miniscule lines of code? Or are you up to your neck in the latest project management software?

Do you have clients who expect miracles overnight? Or do clients not really fully understand what you're doing for them or why you're doing it? Or do you have some clients who frankly don't pay you well? Or are you often waiting on responses from your clients to get things done?

Do you need to do 100 things first before you can enjoy a week away? Do you still get client messages anyway? Or do you know that if you took off 2 months there wouldn't be a business to come back to? Or do you need constant free or cheap leads?

Do you get fired if you do the job too well? Or are you the first one to get blamed when there aren't enough sales? Or do you generate a bunch of leads for clients who can't convert them anyway? Or do you have clients who can't answer their phone properly to save their life?

Do you feel like sometimes you have to take any client just to manage your cash flow situation? Do you sometimes have to take the next client with a credit card and a pulse only to regret it later? Do you feel like you need their money?

Do you ever find yourself at lame ass conferences doing the dog and pony show? Do you have a calendar that's filled with the monotony of sales calls? Or do you ever have 90 things all 90% finished?

Do your clients hand you a broken funnel, a broken message, a broken offer, and a broken website and expect it to work instantly? Or do you know your campaign needs months of testing to dial it in but your clients just don't give you enough time to make it work?

Do you constantly feel like you're explaining the same things over and over and over? Or is yet another client shocked when they get their ad bill and they aren't overnight rich yet?

It's a pretty thankless job, wouldn't you say?

What If Your Agency Could Be Different?

What if it didn't have to be like that? What if there was a better and easier way?

What if you could have the benefits of the monthly recurring cash flow and it didn't require you to do all of those things?

What if you had actual time and freedom together? What if you didn't even have to check your email or your phone for days or even weeks at a time?

What if you didn't have to have any meetings at all? What if every client you spoke with was already pre-sold before they even got on the phone with you? What if a 'sales call' was a 3 minute formality where you just processed their credit card over Stripe?

What if you didn't have to put your entire financial livelihood in the hands of the almighty Google or Facebook?

What if you could look at your calendar and see not a single damn thing on it? What if a typical average day had nothing you "have to" do?

What if you had a team of A+ superstars and systems to do almost all of the heavy lifting for you? What if you had systems and processes to ensure everything was done the right way every time? What if your systems could make your life infinitely easier? What if it was better for your clients too?

What if you could carefully choose only the clients who you really vibed with? What if they were as easy as "friends with money" to talk to? What if you only had clients because you really believed in what they were selling? What if together you were making the world a better place? What if you only had fun with your clients?

What if you weren't dependent on ads or SEO in the first place? What if another Google update or ad account shutdown didn't even affect you *at all*?

What if you could quite literally get paid while your drooling head was still asleep on your pillow? What if you worked only when you felt like it? What if you could do most of the work on a notepad on the beach? What if you didn't even have to have a phone or a computer at all? What if not a single message was ever urgent?

What if when you worked once, you got paid for it again and again? What if you only had to sell proven offers to proven buyers? What if that certainty made your job a thousand times easier?

What if you could get every client of yours results within the first 48 hours? What if those results built instant trust and credibility? What if those same clients saw you differently than your competitors? What if they saw you as a partner, investor, or highly skilled consultant instead of as their underlying to boss around?

What if you could do this while traveling around the world? What if you could experience multiple different countries? What if you wake up on a beach in Thailand? What if you could have a delicious butter pastry in France? What if you could see the crystal blue waters in Lake Louise Canada? What if you could actually have a successful agency *and* the time to live a very cool life?

What if you actually had time, space, and leverage to just be? Would you learn a new language? Would you eat some great food? Would you have sex in the middle of the day?

What if your business had almost zero stress? What if you didn't have to "convince" anybody ever? What if you could help your clients completely ethically and honestly? What if you felt good about what you were doing every day?

Most importantly, what if that was *real*? Like really, really *real*. What if that was not only possible… but possible *for you*?

If you've been running an agency for a while, I know that probably sounds unbelievable. Your bullshit detector may be going haywire. If so, that's totally understandable. I used to feel that way too.

I probably would not have believed it either. Except that's been my life and my clients' lives for many years now. We've learned to escape the agency trap of working for money. We've escaped the trap of being subservient to clients. We've escaped having to reinvent the wheel with every new client. We've escaped running an agency that isn't really scalable. We've escaped an agency that creates a tighter electronic leash to your phone and email as you become more successful.

We've escaped running a boring typical agency the way everyone else does it. By using the principles of this book, you will escape it too.

Most people in this world aren't really living. For them, they are only living for the weekend. Others are waiting for retirement before they truly start living.

You don't have to wait 30 years to have a cool life. You don't have to do a bunch of shit you don't want to do so you can *hopefully* experience something cool later.

If you're ready to escape the trap of working for money and being your client's slave, strap yourself in. Inside this book you will find some massive wealth, time, and leverage shortcuts. You're going to discover a new model of running an agency called a "Beyond Agency".

This will reimagine and reinvent everything you've been told that you "have to do".

In applying these principles, you will be able to live on your own terms. Your digital marketing business will work for you instead of you being a prisoner to it. It will actually scale in both freedom and money together. This will allow you the framework to design yourself a really cool life filled with beautiful experiences.

That means doing what you want, when you want, and with who you want, with purpose and passion, and only doing what you are gifted at and love doing. Are you ready to have a successful lifestyle agency?

Real talk: There are other books that will teach you better Facebook ad skills, a better sales script for closing clients, or a better airtight client contract. This book is the premier resource for having an agency that gives you a cool life.

If that's for you, read on.

Chapter 2: The 5 Stages Of Agency Growth

Before we get into how to create a new type of "Beyond Agency", where are you now? Which stage is your agency in *now*?

This is extremely important to you. Because knowing where you are and what you really need is exactly how you move the needle in a big way.

If you've had the same problem in your life for more than 6 months, you are most likely solving the wrong problem. That's what most agency owners are doing. They are unknowingly solving the wrong problems. They are usually addressing a surface level symptom. Without truly understanding the deeper underlying issue, they don't really go anywhere.

One of my clients was doing a cool $1.2 million per year in his business. He wanted to grow further but he was upside down on his cash flow. His employees were getting paid but he wasn't.

His agency was already sucking the life out of him. He was stressed most months that he might not be able to make payroll. He dreaded the idea of laying somebody off because he couldn't figure things out.

He was seriously contemplating just blowing the whole thing up and doing something else. Anything just so he didn't have so many headaches. When you are scaling and upside down on your cash flow situation, it's a tough grind. If you've ever been there, you understand his stress.

Plus his clients demanded things from him all day every day. As he so eloquently described it, "It's like I have 100 different bosses."

It's confusing because he didn't realize that what got him to his current level of success is *different* than the skills needed to get to the next level.

What Got You *Here* Won't Get You *There*.

Is he meant to hire before cash flow could sustain it or should he wait until he had enough clients and then hire quickly? How did the big boys land the million dollar contracts? What sort of margins should he be working towards?

He already built the entire business from zero. He got to his first $10k/month through hard work and sheer determination. At $100k/month, he was already hustling so hard that Gary V would have gotten a massive erection.

Hustle won't unlock the next level. Working harder won't get you another $100k per month. It's not like he can wave a magic wand and add another 12 hours to the day, right?

In fact, he'll only make more when he actually *works less*. He needs teams, processes, people, systems, and leverage. Only a well-oiled machine will allow him to keep scaling or at least cruise on autopilot.

So what do you personally need to get to the next level? You need to know firstly which stage you're in, what your real challenges are, and what are the real problems that need to be fixed.

Stage 1: Freelancer Freddy

What you're doing: Everything. Janitor/CEO/Web Design/etc. You're designing the logos. You're taking the sales calls. You're generating the leads. You're the wordpress guy/gal. You're the one running the campaigns. You're the one emailing clients back when they have a question. In this stage, if you take a month off, there won't be a business to come back to.

What it feels like: Fighting fires all day. Wondering where to get clients from.

What the biggest problem you have is: You're usually wondering how you can get more clients. Your biggest problem is client acquisition.

How to solve it: You need working processes and systems of client generation. You need an irresistible offer. You need something that makes your agency stand out from the noise.

Typical income: $0-20k/month

Stage 2: Small Team Steve

What you're doing: You're still doing much of the work. You're also now also managing people.

What it feels like: Everyone else around me is incompetent. No one does it right but me. It's easier just to do it myself. You carry 10x as much work as anybody else in your agency.

What the biggest problem you have is: Hiring and retaining A+ superstar employees and freelance help. You probably have B and C player help. They're not good enough for you to truly "let go" and trust them to do a good job. It seems only you care about quality.

How to solve it: Need systems for hiring, training, and retaining superstars.

Typical income: $20-50k/month

Stage 3: Mark The Manager

What you're doing: Managing a team. You are a full time manager in support daily of your staff and their issues.

What it feels like: All day long someone asks you, "Hey do you have a minute?" You're interrupted constantly.

What the biggest problem you have is: Managing by firefighting. You are probably 'reactionary' with issues, dealing with them as they come up. You are probably busy doing whatever employees dump in your lap. Every decision depends on you and so you become the bottleneck in your own agency.

How to solve: Manage by benchmarks and fix systems, processes, and procedures. You have to know your numbers and use that to guide your decisions. Your effort needs to be focused in the right place. There are 5 to 10 key performance indicators that define every agency. You have to know those numbers and work at the right problems proactively. Only solving the right problems will move you forward.

Typical income: $50-200k/month

Stage 4: Chuck The CEO

What you're doing: Managing managers. Deciding on high level opportunities.

What it feels like: Finally I get to do the shit I like doing. You're only focused on creative work. You're no longer involved in any "day to day" operations.

What the biggest problem you have is: The quality of your brand slips. Suddenly you have stuff falling through cracks. Your office is "political" and you have cliques. "I heard Joey got promoted because he goes golfing with Debbie."

How to solve: Fall in love with your customers again. Get back to the basics.

Typical income: $200k-500k/month

Stage 5: Franchising Frank

What you're doing: Living like a cuban drug lord.

What it feels like: Constant opportunity overload. People are constantly bringing you new opportunities, investments, and ideas.

What the biggest problem you have is: Cloning your systems from location to location. Finding A+ players gets harder and harder.

How to solve: I legit have no idea. I have never been in this stage. Though I do have a few colleagues, friends, and clients that have shared their experiences here.

Typical income: Rapper money.

As for you, you probably don't want a rapper mansion that's worthy of 10 minutes on MTV Cribs. You probably don't want to have an international brand franchise either.

You probably just want to have a really good "lifestyle" agency. One where you can earn 7 figures or more on your laptop on the beach. One where you actually have time to be with the people you love most.

These stages are here to help you get clear and then get unstuck. Reread them when you need to. It is a reminder of what is your most important and biggest challenge.

Chapter 3: Solving Your Sales Woes Once And For All

If you're in stage 1 or stage 2, then you probably need more sales. Even if you're past these stages, who doesn't want more sales?

For most freelancers and agency owners, more sales equals more work. Later, we're going to shatter this unhelpful link. We will cover creative ways so that more clients means less work. This will also introduce you to something called a "Beyond Agency". It will actually make your business life far more stress free. Before we get there though, let's uplevel your sales and profits.

What's the *one thing* that makes it really easy for clients to give you money?

Contrary to popular belief, it is *not* becoming better at selling. You don't need the 247 step shiny objection handling sequence. You don't need the 1-2-3 Whizzbamo closing technique (patent pending). You don't need to twist anyone's arm. You don't need to pressure people to do what you want them to do. In fact, you don't need to coerce anyone at all.

"It's about the offer stupid." - Marketing legend Dan Kennedy

The most important thing is to get your offer really, really *dialed in*. You must have something totally irresistible; something that your market desperately wants and needs.

It must be something that only you can provide for them. It should be unique to you and your agency. Most of all, it should appeal to the specific type of client you most want to work with. It must be sexy to the right person and irrelevant to all the wrong ones.

Here's the kicker. Most agencies have a shitty "me too" offer. If you could sum up their offer, it looks something like this.

Typical agency offer: "Give me thousands of dollars every month and I'll try and generate some leads for you. You will have to close those leads yourself. I will generate leads by running some ads and/or building some backlinks for you. Eventually after a few months, hopefully you'll make some money. No guarantees though."

In summary, invest lots of money, wait a while, and then no guarantee it will even work.

Now, when you put it like that, do you see anything wrong with that picture? Do you see how that offer would be totally *resistible*? Do you see how it might even turn most people off? Do you see how that's already paddling upstream?

Do you see why that offer needs a massive amount of selling and coercing?

If that's your offer, it gets even worse. It's asking a complete stranger to invest thousands of dollars with a long term commitment. Then they have to wait and see if it will get them a result. In the end, there's no guarantee that it's actually going to work for them. Plus even if you do a great job and generate truckloads of red hot leads, what if they're like most businesses? What if they have no idea how to convert them?

To top it off, you have a million different competitors. Isn't pretty much everybody and their cousin/brother/uncle now a "digital marketing expert"? It's a recipe for disaster. It's an unnecessary steep uphill climb.

The Dreaded Typical Agency Trap

If you run a typical agency with a typical me too offer, you're already behind the 8-ball. A lame offer puts you in very shark-infested waters.

Escaping that means having an offer that is truly different and better. Your success begins and ends with your offer. You can't be another "me too" agency.

Example me too agency: "You do Facebook ads? Well gee golly gosh darn it, me too!"

It's time to get radically outside of the box. Sometimes dramatically improving your offer takes just a small tweak. The stronger and stronger the offer you make, the easier and easier it is to get an instantaneous "yes". The easier and easier you get a "yes", the more you are the one in power.

First A Word About Proposals

Have you ever slaved away 4 hours making a custom proposal, made sure everything was perfect, then sent it off to your prospective client, only to realize a week later they haven't even read it? You wonder how to email them or text them without sounding pushy or desperate.

You end up in chase mode. All you really want is an honest "in" or "out". Instead they act flakey and take forever to get back to you. Most times they disappear and a few times the deal actually pulls through.

Here's the deal. Firstly, most times they asked for a proposal because they weren't convinced. They just wanted to get off the phone without making a decision. Your proposal isn't actually all that important to them. It's also a way for them to intentionally blow you off.

Secondly, most of your clients actually hate reading boring ass proposals. If you want proposals that work, here's one way we've used with big success. Make a 5 minute screen recording video. Your client only really wants to know 4 things.

1. What is the end result going to be?
2. How long will it take?
3. What's it going to cost?
4. How are we going to communicate?

Here's the kicker. Clients love video proposals. They don't actually want to read long technical proposals. They just want it short and to the point. Plus they probably got at least 3 other quotes from your competitors too. They don't want to read their boring proposals either. They just want to know what you're really offering them.

If you want to never have to make a proposal ever again, make your offer unique and better. Imagine the power of having 100 people waiting in line for your offer. With that kind of demand, you can politely say "no" to proposal requests. That's the big secret.

A Great Offer Changes The Landscape

If you've ever sent out cold emails, did outreach on LinkedIn, ran Facebook ads, answered questions in groups, and it didn't work or was just really slow, it was your offer.

The right offer puts you in the driver's seat. You have more people wanting you than you can handle. You become the selector. As the selector, you pick and choose the clients that are the right fit for you. Generally that means they are easy to help, fun to work with, and stay happy with you for a very, very long time. The right clients feel more like "friends with money".

Here's What Pimping An Offer Looks Like...

How much would you pay for a steak dinner? $20 maybe? What if that steak was made by Gordon Ramsay? What if you got to eat it with your celebrity crush? What if you got to eat it on top of the Empire State Building? What if there was also a banquet in your honor?

Does it make sense that a steak dinner, prepared by Gordon Ramsay, on top of the Empire State Building, with your celebrity crush, at a banquet in your honor, is infinitely more irresistible than your average $20 steak dinner? How much do you think someone would pay for *that* steak?

Why is that important? Because we're still talking about a steak dinner. It is essentially the same basic product and service. The offer just got sexier. You don't need to be doing something totally different. It just needs adding some sizzle to it.

Here are a few simple ways to add some sizzle to your offer.

Strategy #1 - Result Guarantees

One of the simplest ways that you can improve your offer is by adding a results guarantee. Naturally, this will put you on the hook to perform. You will need to choose your clients carefully so you can actually deliver.

At the same time, you'll get far more people to say "yes" with a guarantee. I've personally seen guarantees increase sales 2-5x for the exact same agency. This is especially true if nobody else in your industry offers one.

Should you offer a guarantee? It's up to you. What makes sense for you and your industry depends on you. In some niches it will make you dramatically stand out. In others a guarantee is just another 'me too' offer.

Let's first look at the downside. The biggest fear you probably have is the "dreaded refund". What if you sign a client and then they want their money back? It will happen every now and then. However, refunds are actually a lot rarer than most people think. Plus, they can mostly be avoided. It usually happens because you mistakenly worked with somebody you should have said 'no' to.

Now the upside. At the same time, is 2-5x more sales worth a few refunds every now and then? A strong guarantee can be a great start at improving your offer. It can make you stand out from the competition. Many hugely successful agencies were built solely with a guarantee as their primary differentiator.

There is no one offer or guarantee that works in every niche and industry. What is "new" in one niche is old hat in another. What works for you will depend on what is already being offered at large in your niche and industry.

If you are the first one doing a guarantee, it has a profound effect. If others are doing, it will just be another "me too" offer. Use guarantees wisely and strategically.

Strategy #2 - Guaranteed Appointments

Another thing that's working really well is selling guaranteed appointments. This works particularly well with local businesses and other service providers. It also works really well for online coaches and consultants.

Nobody really wants to buy "leads" from you. Because even when they get leads, most clients won't know how to turn them into anything meaningful.

If you've ever had a client who sucks at answering the phone, you know exactly what I'm talking about.

Your clients will find you more valuable if you help them to bridge the gap by selling appointments instead of generic leads. Sometimes that means you just have to send a few follow up emails and add a scheduling app at the bottom of the emails.

Is that little tweak worth more sales and more happy clients? We think so. Better yet, how can you create it once and reuse it to get paid again and again? (Hint: We cover more about "leveraging" in the 30 year wealth shortcut chapter. More on that later.)

Strategy #3 - Specific Desirable Lead Types

Your clients don't value their customers equally. Think 80-20. You can offer your clients specific customers that they value a lot more.

For example, what's more valuable to a dentist - a $100 check up or a $35,000 set of veneers? What's more valuable to an online coach - an $8 webinar registration or a $25,000 mastermind client? What's more valuable to an ecommerce client - a $20 plastic trinket or a $99/month recurring supplement package?

Generally speaking, it's no more work for you to generate one lead versus the other. You might as well focus on the most valuable impact you can make for a client. You might as well offer the most desirable leads you can deliver.

Strategy #4 - Combine Value

Most of your clients have more problems than just "leads". Even if they get a phone call, strategy session, or booking, what normally happens? They probably can't close them. Once they get a client, what happens? They won't know how to turn that person into repeat business and a referral.

One of the things we did in our lawyer agency was to give more. We ran Facebook ads like everyone else. However, we also included phone training. The training included example phone calls from top law firms in the country. They used this to uplevel their staff to convert like pros.

We also gave them referral materials. When clients came in the door, they now had the ability to multiply their clients with a few fancy business cards. This was inherently more valuable than just "leads".

When your offer stands out from the noise, even if it's just in a small way, it will make you the only source of what you do. If you're a lawyer who are you going to keep around?

A. The guy who can get a few cheap FB leads?

B. Or the guy who can get you leads, train your staff to convert like a world class firm, help you turn your new clients into referrals, and sent you a custom engraved set of knives just because you love to cook?

Person B wins every time. Combine value and you'll have more 10 year clients and less 3-6 month clients like everybody else.

Combining value helped the lawyers to be able to close the leads they got and multiply their client base. It was just a printed phone script, a few business cards, and a few video modules.

No one else offered that. That's where you want to be. In your own category of one. Where you are the only one who offers what you offer. Where you are the most valuable solution regardless of price.

If you never want to have to make proposals and chase people again, add more value than everyone else. One of the easiest ways to do that is just to make your offer do more.

The best part is that it doesn't mean extra work for you. You can make a deal for the extras. How hard is it to find someone with an already great course on phone support and negotiate a deal to give to each client?

Strategy #5 - Beyond Agency Revenue Sharing

By far the best way to make a killer offer is to partner or invest. How does it work? You help them increase their sales for a percentage of the excess revenues. Here's what that sounds like to a potential client.

"Would you be interested in adding an extra revenue source and you don't have to pay me unless it works? Would you be open to a small test campaign to show you it works?"

It's an easy "yes". Plus you can get a far greater share of results if you can handle being paid second. Usually it just means waiting 7-10 days for your cut. Most people will happily pay you 30-50% of profits.

This strategy might sound complicated and expensive, but it's actually really dog shit simple. We'll cover this in more detail later in the book.

What Is The Most Important Thing You Can Do?

Remember the 5 stages of agency growth from earlier? If you're reading this book, your agency is most likely in stage 1 or 2. That means your single biggest challenge is upgrading your offer.

You can now breathe a deep sigh of relief. Because it means most things that people tell you are important really aren't. There are an infinite number of ways to make your offer better, beyond just what's covered in this book.

You don't need to be obsessed with your logo. You don't need to trick Google into quickly ranking you #1. You don't need to get your webinar just right. You can even hit $100k/month without having a website. Most of these things are a waste of your valuable time.

In fact, I have found that even today in today's busy world, through cold outreach, sending three or four messages with the right offer, we can pick up a client within an hour. When your offer is so "irresistible", you don't need so much tech.

After all, what's a "funnel" but a well-crafted way to deliver an offer? What's a website but an automated tool to deliver your offer? What's a Facebook ad but another offer? What is a "sales call" but 60 minutes of talking to make an offer?

If you can't sell your offer in a few short sentences, why would all the bells and whistles make an unsexy offer sexy? It can't. So before we add complexity to your offer with funnels and websites, shouldn't we get the most important piece just right?

That means before you get into the 1-2-3 Whizzbang Gizmo Funnel technique, get the offer right. This is your biggest leverage point. Hit a homerun here. Like Dan Kennedy says, "It's about the offer stupid."

Also, I've discovered a way for getting new clients every week without Facebook ads, SEO, webinars, or complicated funnels. I love to share it with you for free. Download the free resources at beyondagencyprofits.com.

Chapter 4: The Agency Model Reimagined

Now it's time to reinvent the game for you. We're about to shatter the paradigm that most freelancers and agency owners operate under. You should be pretty stoked about that. Because it's an artificial box they put themselves into without knowing it.

Here's a big, big shift you must make immediately. Most agency models can be summed up like this:

Pay First. Results Later. (Hopefully.)

But what if there ain't no cash flow to pay you and wait? Guess what? They can't be "investing" in you right now.

Even if there is cash flow, you're probably a big risk to them. What if they have the cash and frankly just don't trust you? What if too many slick talking salespeople have conned them before?

Isn't it asking a lot of a stranger to invest a big chunk of cash and wait? Especially if they can't tell you apart from every other "digital marketing expert" out there?

Now here's what that means to you.

You Must Be Bakin' Your Folks A Bigger Pie.

Which of these is much more likely to get automatic yeses?

Option 1:

How about you pay me $2500 per month plus 10% of ad spend first...

...and later in a few months, I'll get you some leads that you have to convert yourself and hopefully you eventually make some money?

Option 2:

If you're cool with it, I'd like to take your ingredients you're not using in the cupboard and bake you a bigger pie immediately...

...and then only after you're fat full of pie, would you be cool with giving me a big fat slice too?

Hopefully you were noddin' along with Option 2.

Because there's a moral to this story. Be a source of cash flow to businesses right now. Bake pies first. Get your slices second. Usually about 7-10 days later. Then take a big fat slice for yourself.

Hint: If they've already got all the ingredients ready to go, a warm hot oven, a recipe book in the cupboard with a few proven winning recipes, and a database of known pie eaters, pie eaters that they probably haven't even contacted in years, you might just be sitting on a virtual gold-mine-o'-pie. Ya dig? (No pies were harmed during the making of this book.)

That only describes about 75% of the businesses in existence. You should be able to find a few.

Beyond Agency vs Traditional Agency

What's the difference and why should you care? Here's how the two look different. Which of these agencies would you prefer?

Strategy:

Traditional Agency - Trade Google or Facebook ad services for money or backlink building and SEO rankings for money every month. Deliver leads that they must close themselves. No help is offered in closing those leads. It is 100% their responsibility to convert them.

Beyond Agency - Launching quick reusable campaigns to bring clients quick easy cash. Trade results for fees. Prefer acquiring and controlling undervalued assets and getting paid cash over just earning monthly cash alone. Most of the customers are pre-closed for clients.

Pay Structure:

Traditional - Monthly fee (sometimes plus ad spend). Typically $500/month to $7500/month depending on your tier of clients. Most people are on the lower end of the scale.

Beyond Agency - Profit share of 30-50%. Typically $10k/month per client with choosing clients correctly.

Mindset:

Traditional - Trade monthly lead generation services for money. Often ends up in a "client-underling" relationship. They will see you as their employee. You typically try to get a long term contract to keep them as long as possible. Most clients typically last 3-12 months.

Beyond Agency - Become a "micro investor" into a client to see if they have easy untapped profits. You go steady with the winners. You get a share of the profits you generate (30-50%) 7-10 days later. Most clients typically last a few days if they're not a good fit or for years and years if it benefits everyone involved.

What You're Doing:

Traditional - Building funnels, tweaking websites, spending time in an ad manager, using reporting software, and/or building backlinks. You spend a lot of time inside the tech. It takes a lot of micro testing in order to get a client a result. Often you will have a lot of proposals, reports, and unnecessary meetings. Because you are working on the area clients pay the most attention to (their front end), you will most likely be watched like a hawk. Your every move will be scrutinized heavily.

Beyond Agency - Running a series of copy and paste email and direct mail campaigns. Uses leverage by reusing campaigns already proven to work. We don't reinvent the wheel. No meetings, reports, or advanced tech is required. Most campaigns work from day one without any testing.

Client Problem You Solve:

Traditional - This is two fold. Clients always "think" they need more traffic but almost always their offers, funnels, and messaging are broken. They actually need help converting their traffic too. Lots of split-testing and time needed to dial their system in. You are almost always hired to "bring traffic" when in reality you are actually "making their shit sell".

Beyond Agency - Cash flow. You help clients get a bump in cash flow by utilizing their own underutilized resources. Often it's as simple as following up with past customers and offering them more of the same.

How You Help Them:

Traditional - Through a series of ads or rankings, you get people to their website or landing pages. This (hopefully) gets strangers to buy from them. Usually they don't know what to do with the leads you get them and they almost always feel they are paying too much. You go after the hardest customers first; new people who have never heard of them before. This takes time.

Beyond Agency - You help them sell more to the customers they have. You accomplish this with simple gratitude campaigns. You go after the easiest customers first; the ones who already bought from them and are happy about it. This works almost immediately.

Types of Clients You Have:

Traditional - It is usually based on who you think you can get. There are occasional pros who can command top prices with the top end of the market. Typically it's whatever client you can get. A credit card and a pulse are enough qualifications. You rarely turn clients away.

Beyond Agency - You carefully choose the people that are the easiest to win with. By choosing, you don't go for most clients. You exclude most clients who are more headaches and opt for the low hanging fruit.

Your Offer:

Traditional - Give me money first, wait a few months while I dial in your leads, and maybe then you'll see some results. You are responsible for converting your own leads. It's a tough yes.

Beyond Agency - Let me run a little test campaign and I'll know in a few days whether we can generate profit for you. If it works, I'd like a share of the profits. If it generates profit, I would like to continue working together. It's almost an automatic yes.

How Client Sees You:

Traditional - Most clients see you as an "expense" until proven otherwise. Especially in a difficult financial situation, you will be the first to go if they have to cut back. Usually 3-6 months minimum is needed to dial your process in. You may need longer still if you do SEO. "They generally think, "You work for me." They also compare you to every Tom, Dick, and Harry who also runs Facebook or Google ads or does SEO.

Beyond Agency - You are seen as a source of cash flow and an investor/partner. They generally think, "You are an invaluable consultant who pays for themselves." They don't know anyone else who does what you do.

Who Takes On The "Risk":

Traditional - The client accepts 100% of the risk. They pay first. They hope for results later. It's why they often want many reports and meetings to justify you are moving them towards the goal. Until the results come, they feel pretty uneasy about the situation. Often they have been burned by a smooth-talking salesperson in the past. They worry a lot about ad expenses and your process not working.

Beyond Agency - You assume and manage the risk strategically. This is because you're an entrepreneur and you are far more risk tolerant. You choose the right situations wisely and test small before committing to anything big. You manage risk wisely. You do this by maximizing the upside if you are right and minimizing the downside if you are wrong. Imagine a coin that lands tails costs you $10 and if it lands heads, you get $1000. You keep flipping that coin even if it's been tails 7 times in a row. You take on high upside low risk deals.

Internal State Of Being:

Traditional - This is only based on my own experience. Your experience may differ. Often you feel guilty if a client has paid you and you haven't gotten them results yet. You worry a lot at night about delivering on the promises you made. You are doing your best trying to keep everyone happy. Also, if a client wants a meeting or a phone call, you feel obligated to say "yes". If a client asks for a proposal, meeting, or report, you almost feel like you have to. You feel like you have to check your phone or email all the time. Clients have lots of seemingly urgent requests. I used to check my email 20+ times per day. It was a virtual "electronic leash".

Beyond Agency - You don't start a relationship with any overt big promises made or asking for anything first. Ergo you have no "bosses". You feel very in control of the client relationship. You spend a lot of your time figuring out how to add value to their customers. You don't feel the need to make reports, proposals, or have meetings that are not necessary. Your clients tend to feel more like friends and partners. You probably check your email once every few days. You virtually never receive an urgent request for a call, meeting, or proposal.

When The Relationship Ends:

Traditional - Either you rocked their results and they don't need you anymore or they expected a miracle and it didn't happen. Usually the relationship is over in 3-12 months and clients generally leave unhappy. There are some exceptions but typically they will leave disappointed. Sometimes clients are their own worst enemy. They will blame you for what they did or didn't do. Managing expectations is crucial to your continued success.

Beyond Agency - You decide it wasn't a fit after a small test and wish them well on their journey. Nobody is mad or disappointed at the other party. It's like a first date where you mutually agree not to have a second date.

Client Expectations:

Traditional - Clients expect results quicker than it usually takes. They generally believe generating new clients is "binary". It either works or it doesn't. This means they don't have patience to test what they need to test. Often because they don't give you working offers, funnels, messaging, etc. Often they hire you when they "need" it to work. There can be a "desperation energy" present. It can put immense pressure on you to deliver miracles fast. We as agency owners also generally do a poor job of letting them know the time, cost, results, and communication. Thinking they already know what to expect is a critical mistake.

Beyond Agency - You have almost no expectations because you're not really promising anything. Anything you generate is seen as a bonus. If you win, they are stoked. If you lose, they didn't expect much anyway. Expectations are still important but you can get away with not setting any. You have far more wiggle room for errors.

If you want our template for setting boss-like expectations go to our free Facebook group called

"Beyond Agency Profits". If you're not already there, get your butt inside. I've discovered a way to get new clients every week without Facebook ads, SEO, webinars, or complicated funnels. I love to share it with you for free. It's all inside the group.

By the way, neither agency type is right or wrong. It depends on what you want. There are pros and cons to both.

The Biggest Downsides

The biggest downside to a Beyond Agency is you are the one taking ALL the risk. If you don't know how to choose the right clients, this can be catastrophic. You will do a lot of work and never get paid for it. There are a lot of pitfalls in choosing the right clients. There are too many to list here. You manage that risk by testing small by taking clients on a small 'first date'. You will learn more by working with them.

The biggest downside to a traditional agency is clients see you as "working for them". They'll want lots of meetings, reports, and proposals. This makes it really hard to be "free". The more success your agency has, the more it will become like a "high-paying job". If you just want the "laptop lifestyle" and don't really love building backlinks or dicking around all day inside an ad manager, it will prevent you from really being "free".

I used to always feel like my phone and my laptop were my "electronic leash". A traditional agency is one of the hardest businesses to completely automate and outsource. A few of the most successful agency owners on Earth have told me "it's not scalable". Though it absolutely can be done, it is by no means easy.

The Biggest Upsides

The biggest upside to a Beyond Agency is that it has unlimited leverage. Campaigns that work for one client are easy to slightly modify and use again and again. Rinse, lather, repeat. You get to "do work once" and get paid for it over and over. It has a higher upside. You aren't reinventing the wheel with each and every client. This creates leverage that makes it easy to grow.

The upside to a traditional agency is you end up with monthly cash flow that adds up. Just a few good clients means you'll earn more than most people do in a high-paying job. In my first agency in 2007, it took me 5 clients at $1k/month to earn $52k/year. I was beyond thrilled to not need a "real job" ever again. It doesn't take a lot of those deals to move the needle.

Of course, you can do hybrid deals as well. You can get creative and use aspects of a traditional agency and also have profit sharing opportunities. There is no box and you can do whatever makes sense for you.

Which is right for you? It just depends what you want. If you love doing ads and building backlinks or you are not a big fan of risk, go the traditional agency route. It will make more sense for you. If you just want to help people, live free, and earn a great living, a Beyond Agency is a better path. The choice is yours.

Chapter 5: Absolutely Rocking Your Client Results

Imagine each and every client was blown away with the results you got for them. They thanked you, asked if you could do more to help them, and referred you to their colleagues and friends. It's totally possible.

How do you get clients results? There are only ever three ways you can help your client have a bigger payday.

1. Get more new people.
2. Help them increase transaction size.
3. Sell more frequently to their customers.

Here is something absolutely critical you must fully integrate. Everybody *thinks* they need "new people".

They don't.

Old cash pays the same as new cash. Old cash is a heckuva lot easier too. Old cash works a lot faster too. Old cash is tried and true.

Plus, more importantly for you, getting new people is where all the competition is. It's also the hardest way to get results for your clients. Over 99% of agencies are obsessed with getting new people.

That's because that's what most clients directly ask for. However, it's important to understand that "new" is always the least efficient way.

All the real money is made in retaining and upselling. Dan Kennedy says, "The purpose of making a sale is to acquire a customer." Most people have it all completely ass backwards.

"The Purpose Is Not To Make A Sale, But To Get A Customer. Peeps Sell Their Products Or Services And Throw Their Customers Away." - Travis Sago

Most people don't realize it, but the most powerful asset in any business is *the relationship with the customer.* Your customer list is your gold. Nurture the relationship and you always have something and someone to sell to forever.

Let's illustrate the power of this principle. Imagine you just signed a new client named Dave who runs a typical American restaurant. Naturally, Dave wants to make more money.

The first thing Dave thinks is "I need more new customers". Remember though, new customers is *just one possible way* to increase Dave's cash flow. It's just an idea. If Dave wants to achieve results quickly and easily, it's also the wrong approach.

My last girlfriend used to be a real Groupon junkie. If you're not familiar with Groupon, it is an app that can save you money through using virtual coupons. Much like a physical coupon book, you can use Groupon to get deals of up to 50-70%. Lots of restaurants use them to attract new people.

My girlfriend and I would go to all these new restaurants because of Groupon. We were new customers, exactly like Dave wanted. More often than not, we would try Dave's food once and leave.

It really sucks for all the Daves out there because he gives 50% off the regular price. On top of that, he gives another 50% fee to Groupon. Dave is lucky to get ¼ of his normal price. On a $50 meal for two, Dave might collect $12.50. Dave still has food cost, overhead, and staff to pay for.

Dave is losing money to try and bring in a new customer in the door. It gets worse. *Dave actually has a much deeper problem.*

Because what Dave really lacked was the ability to bring his customers back and add more value. In visiting over 50 restaurants, no one had a single strategy to retain and upsell us. They just "hoped" we liked our cheap meal so much that we came back on our own.

Hope is not a strategy. Like most customers, we just got busy and forgot. Even the restaurants we liked didn't earn back our business.

Dave Doesn't Know What Dave Actually Needs

Think about this. Because you're the one responsible for improving Dave's business. Most of the Daves of the world would hire you and tell you that what they need is "more new customers". That would only make the *real problem* worse.

Imagine instead that you intervened and helped Dave be more strategic. You asked Dave if they were open to trying something small together to see if you could bake him a bigger pie. Dave likes pie for himself with no risk so he agreed to a small test.

At each table you put a sign that said, "Want 10% off your meal today? Join our special VIP customer list. Just 'text VIP to 12345' and you'll get a 10% virtual coupon for your meal today. Thanks for coming into Dave's American restaurant." Even better, you raised Dave's prices 10% so it didn't even cost anything to give a discount.

Next imagine that each week you texted out new offers. Free dessert this week. Lunch special next week. Half price appetizer next week. You kept giving us customers endless reasons to come back.

You're just creating a simple offer to come back. It's no more work than 2 lines in a text message.

If you did this right, we now start to come back once per week. Of course, it wouldn't just work on only us. Now Dave has regulars who are dropping in once per week. Dave is stoked.

Dave smartly built a list of his most valued customers. You controlled it. That means Dave is no longer dependent on any third party service like Groupon, Google, or Facebook. Dave doesn't need all that ongoing ad cost just to chase the new girl at the dance.

Now imagine you helped Dave again to add some extra value upsells. You came up with more and more simple reasons to make Dave's restaurant cool. Some ideas worked and some didn't.

Dave offered extra drinks. Then he offered a 3 day cooking class. Then he offered to come watch a great local band. Dave got some specialty cookware from the local restaurant supplier. He created a take out lunch special that was ready for pick up in 10 minutes for busy professionals. Dave catered local private weddings and special events. The possibilities for him are limitless.

Imagine because you kept adding value, we also spent twice as much money each week. Again, we weren't the only happy customers. Other people did this too. It became the new normal.

Here's Where The Money Math Gets Interesting

Most of the Groupon restaurants we went to only 1x. A few earned a second visit. None of them turned us into repeat customers. Nobody upsold us anything. All in all, we spent less than $50 total with every single restaurant. That's a real world "case study".

Imagine instead those Daves got your help. Imagine you focused on those two leverage points - upselling and creating regular repeat buyers. You ignored their false belief that they needed more new business.

Because you did a good job, we would spend $100 per week for the next year. In just one year, we would spend 100x more than the average one-and-done customer. At $100 per week, we spent $5200 for the year. That's just in year one. What if we stay as happy customers for 10 years?

Now let's look at the money math once again. A single visit customer is worth $12.50 to Dave now. That's after he gets violently raped and pillaged by Groupon. A weekly customer, with a little extra value added, is worth $5200 per year. Which would Dave rather have - $12.50 one time customer or $100 every week?

Do you get the difference between a one-and-done $12.50 customer and a $5200/year customer for life? What does that do for your client Dave?

See the bigger picture here. Because you may be thinking this doesn't apply to you because your clients aren't restaurants. This doesn't just apply to restaurants.

This principle is true in every business, including yours and your client's. Even if you never work with a restaurant, this principle still applies to you. Your business operates under the same principles. Because all businesses operate under the same principles.

New, New, New Business = Hard Work, Low Pay
Retain, Upsell, & Value = Easy Work, High Pay

Dave doesn't know what he really needs. Because what businesses *really* struggle with is actually making offers to upsell and keep their customers. Here's the kicker for you. It's way easier to retain and add value. It's just that nobody thinks to do it.

After all, what's harder - getting a stranger to get dressed, drive in their car, sit down and wait 30 minutes, and try some food they've never tried? Or offer a drink special to Dave's customer sitting there right in front of him? Customers are easier because the relationship is already there. The sales hurdle is much lower.

Even businesses that seem "transactional" on the surface aren't. It's only because the owners treat their customers like a transaction. It's only because those Daves see their customers like another name and number.

It's always the relationship that really matters. That is the key leverage point with which you yield your magic.

What If My Client's Biz Is Only 'One Time'?

There is no such thing as a "one time sale" business. It just seems that way.

Lots of personal injury lawyers used to tell me their business was transactional. Though, it's actually not.

On the surface it made sense. "My clients don't need me unless they've been in a car accident. That's why my business is transactional. Once they've used our service, there isn't anything else we can do."

After working with the top lawyers in the world I noticed a pattern. The most successful lawyers always marketed to their past clients for referrals. They never stopped building that relationship.

This meant a big difference. They would acquire one client through advertising and that one client would turn into 2-10 referral clients over the next 10 years. Those new referral clients didn't require expensive ad costs to be acquired. Those referrals only happened intentionally because they kept investing their resources into those relationships. Even long after their "transaction" was done, they followed up.

Not surprisingly, those lawyers had far more money to spend on marketing to get new clients. Because the better they were at retaining and adding value, the more money they had on the front end to get new people.

Secrets Of The Big Shot Lawyers

I got a chance to work with all types of lawyers, including the less marketing savvy ones. I would often hear new lawyers say, "Lawyer X spends millions on TV ads. I could never afford that." They always assumed their "secret" was that they had deeper pockets.

This was somewhat true. They did have deeper pockets. However, it was only true because they continued to add value and upsell. Having every client come with more business gave them a spending advantage.

Later I got to consult with that top Lawyer X. He was always willing to spend everything he had to get a client. He would literally spend $6000 to get a $6000 client. He did that because he knew every client would bring 2-10 clients later. He knew those referrals did not have an advertising expense.

He saw the bigger picture. He could spend more on his front end because he had a sophisticated back end. Because he was better at retention and adding value, he could outspend everyone only focused on "new". Money goes where it is most easily welcomed.

Being Strategic > Being Transactional

Most businesses sell the product or service and throw the customer away. The purpose of the sale is to get the customer. The first sale should be a hello, not a goodbye.

Now back to your clients. What happens with your clients who really believe that they need 'new' business? What happens when that's what they're willing to pay for? Well you almost have to politely ignore their opinion. If they knew how to solve their problem, they would have already solved it.

They don't actually need more new. They just think 'new' is what will solve their cash flow problems. Adding more "new business" is like pouring water into a leaky bucket. It will just show you all the holes in your bucket.

Chasing "New" Is The Wrong Business To Be In

The more your agency helps clients retain and upsell, the more you can generate immediate results. You will generate faster results and for longer.

When you are the one generating results at will, you get to pick and choose who you want to work with.

Later we will discuss using the right strategy so you will also generate a controllable, leverageable asset. We'll cover why getting assets is a 30 year wealth shortcut.

My $100,000 Client Accident

I wish I could tell you I discovered this next secret because I'm some sort of all-knowing marketing genius. In reality, it was a happy accident that only Bob Ross could fully appreciate. I discovered how much easier and more powerful retaining and upselling is.

One of my clients is a lawyer named Carl in South Carolina. We were running Facebook ads for Carl. I knew that we had spent probably $7,000 - 8,000 in ad spend over 2 and ½ months. When you added in our fee, he had invested somewhere around $14-15,000 in total. I was feeling really stressed out because we hadn't gotten results for him.

At the same time, I was speaking at an event for a big personal injury lawyer organization. We had an intimate little internet marketing bootcamp in Atlanta, Georgia. It was a 3 day event and I was presenting for about 50% of the event. About 20 lawyers were scheduled to be there. We would all be close enough to rub shoulders and stare each other in the eyes.

Carl had bought himself a ticket. I was filled with dread at the thought of seeing him. I was stressed because I hadn't gotten him any results. I was sure he would tell everybody that I'm a fraud. "Don't listen to this guy. He doesn't even know how to run ads. He wasted $15k of my money."

I was prepared for the worst. Lynch mob. Torches. Savage beatings. My death would be short and abrupt.

Except my execution never came. Much to my surprise, Carl greeted me with a giant excited bear hug.

Carl is a big boy and I'm a skinny Canadian. There was nowhere to go to escape that enveloping bear hug. The first thing he said to me, "Do you know I made $100,000 from that campaign?"

I was downright shocked. My jaw was on the floor. A hundred grand? I thought it couldn't be true. I was watching his ads like a hawk. Every day I was tracking his numbers and I was sure we weren't making him money.

Still confused, I thought about it for a second longer. I was in his ad manager on Facebook every single day. We were tracking everything. I knew he had invested significantly with us and we still had nothing to show for it. I was agonizing over my lack of results daily. I was a hundred percent sure our ads had not made his phone ring. Nothing was working yet.

Carl snapped me out of it. "Yeah remember that little referral campaign you sent? I got three clients. One of them is a really big case. It's going to take a couple months to settle, but I'm going to make about a hundred grand."

Honestly, I had totally forgotten about our referral campaign. One of the challenges working with lawyers is that I couldn't really run Google ads for most of them. Of the 100 most expensive keywords on Google, 78 of them are lawyer keywords.

When you're paying $200 per click, a beginning lawyer can get 5-10 clicks before their monthly ad budget is gone. We were running Facebook ads because they were a lot more affordable. The problem was they took longer to work, especially in this niche. We couldn't really target people who had been in a car accident through Facebook ads. On top of it, Facebook doesn't let you just say, "Hey have you been injured in an accident?"

I knew we needed some time to get his funnel working. As a way to give him a quick little bump, I decided to send out a really simple "referral campaign" to his past clients.

The campaign wasn't meant to save the world. I just wanted to get him a client or two so it would pay for the ads. I figured if he had a client or two, he would trust us. I was not trying to create a "Beyond Agency". I just didn't want him to cancel his ad campaigns right away.

Eureka! Hot diggity! The Campaign Worked!

Carl was over the moon! Here I was busting my ass testing hundreds of targeting, copy, and ad creatives. I was desperately trying to make his phone ring. Instead a few poorly worded emails made him 6 figures in a couple days. *It couldn't be that easy, could it?*

Turns out it can be that easy. I realized that it's way easier to help people multiply what's already working. It's way easier to add value and retain.

What did we actually do? The referral campaign was a 4 part email sequence. Our little referral campaign went like this. "Dear past client, thank you so much for being a past client. We appreciate you. I know we don't reach out enough. We just want you to know we want to be your trusted advisor for life. That's why we have a toll free phone number. If you or anybody you know have a legal question, we're happy to answer them for free. If we can't help you, we'll find you somebody who can. This is just a special VIP service that we're offering to you as our valued client. Call us first. Once again, it's free."

It wasn't brilliant but simplicity worked. In fact, simple almost always works better. The reason it worked is because businesses are notoriously bad at marketing to their past customers and clients.

In Carl's case, he had almost 25 years of clients that *he had never once reached out to*. He had twenty five years of happy clients who just needed a gentle nudge.

It's not like we discovered a unicorn. It's not at all uncommon. Only about 1% of lawyers have contacted their past clients. The few that do just sent a boring legal newsletter. Less than 0.1% have done it correctly.

Most times businesses think, "They already bought my thing. I don't know what else I would sell them." Celebrate! Because that belief will make you a lot of money.

Therein Lies The Secret:
Say Thank You + Add Value

It's easy for you to just keep it simple. Because all you have to do is say "thank you" and offer their customers some kind of extra value. That's it. It doesn't need to be any more complicated than that. No funnels. No 12-step webinar complete with retargeting sequence.

Imagine how you can help your clients make a hundred thousand dollars too. The other beautiful benefit is that the result is almost instantaneous. They don't have to wait months and months of paying for ads to hopefully get a result. If you offer SEO, they usually have to wait even longer.

In 48 hours, they know that your stuff works. If it doesn't work, that's useful information too. It usually means they haven't been treating their people well for a long time. In which case, you dodged a bullet. You don't want clients who don't treat their clients well. You don't want businesses who people would not go back to for a second helping.

In a Beyond Agency, that's why you try a first date before committing fully to them. It's for your benefit as much as theirs. You don't want to get married to deadbeat clients before they've earned your trust.

Offer Their Biggest And Best

This strategy works even more powerfully if you can sell their highest end services.

For example, if you were working with a local dentist, getting a few extra $25,000 cosmetic patients is going to do more for him than getting more new $100 checkups. If you have a coach or consultant, selling a package of three calls for $100 isn't going to be the same as if you get somebody in their $12,000 a year mastermind.

Ideally you want to say thank you and offer their biggest packages. What you'll find in doing that is they're actually pretty easy to sell. Because if they've done their job right, their customers already like, know, and trust them. The relationship is there.

If you can't think of what else to offer, ask for referrals. If you want to generate referrals for yourself and your client, it follows the same process. The easiest way is to say thank you and offer extra value.

For example, one of my clients built a 7 figure Facebook ad agency at 17 years old. They sent their clients a personalized Facebook message that said, "I appreciate you. If you have somebody else who has a Facebook ad account, I'd be happy to give them a free account audit. This audit will give them a couple of ways to improve their ads. Usually we can save them 10-20% of their cost in just 10 minutes. There's no obligation. If they want to work with us, we will work hard to make you look good. Even if they don't work with us, they'll get some value out of the audit. The free audit will give them a couple of good ideas that'll help them lower their costs. We would normally charge $500 for this type of consultation. It's just my way of saying thank you."

That's the power of saying thank you and adding strategic value. Most times we make it more complicated than it needs to be. It doesn't require long, complicated funnels. In most cases, funnels are trying to pour more water into an already leaky bucket. Getting results means adding more value to the relationships that are already there.

Inside every business there is an existent flow. Don't try and create flow where it does not yet exist. Harness the flow that is already there. You can get these templates for free by entering your email at beyondagencyprofits.com. Before you read the next chapter, be sure to grab yours.

Chapter 6: Being In 100% Control Of Your Client Relationships

The First Agency Evolution

Around 2012, we first tried a new agency model. We had gotten really good at ranking in Google. It was a lot more "grey hat", but we realized we could rank videos very easily.

We were mostly keeping this strategy to ourselves because we never liked any link strategy that might get a client in trouble. Once we got our videos ranking, they generated phone calls. We would then rent the phone calls to relevant businesses.

We fumbled and bumbled through it and made lots of mistakes. But overall, the idea was a win. Why? Because it meant a few things.

1. We Could Choose Easy Wins.

Before we tried this, SEO was a long tedious process. We had to try and get clients number 1 for all their most difficult keywords. Now we only picked fights we knew we could win quickly.

We no longer had to go after very difficult keywords just because our client "wanted to be number 1". We could sometimes rank a video #1 in a few days. How? Because we just avoided difficult 12 month ranking battles altogether. We only chose easy keywords to rank.

Plus we could try lots of things to rank faster that might normally get a client in hot water. Admittedly, part of it included spammy automated backlinks. Sorry Google.

At the end of the day, we controlled the client flow. The ranking and video were our assets after all. When we wanted more, we could just make another video.

2. We Didn't "Work" For Anybody.

Before we had lots of "client-underling" relationships. This time around we had no boss. This meant no reports, no pointless meetings, and no accountability. We controlled the relationship 100%.

After signing a client, I was no longer tethered to my email and phone. Before they were hiring us to try to get to number one in Google. Now they weren't hiring us to get a result. We already had the result. They wanted a piece of the results that we already controlled.

3. And Most Importantly, It Was *Leverageable*.

If a video worked one place, with a little minor tweak it worked somewhere else. We could basically use the same video in 100's of different markets. We could use it in the same market for different keywords.

We didn't have to reinvent the wheel month after month and month. This was a big upgrade. Because before we were constantly trying to turn client's broken funnels into winners. Before every client situation was unique. Now it was copy and paste. What worked for one roofing company in Detroit worked for another roofing company in Boston.

We had leverage that we had never had before. That's what a Beyond Agency is really about at its core. Do something once and let it work again and again for you.

Since then, we've helped other agency owners and freelancers to change their approach in their own journey. Let's talk a little about the results.

Dan Signed A $482k Deal

Dan My clients think I'm just a nice northern Christian boy, think I should mail em' hannukah cards this year? 😄 deep south Gents.

"Feel, felt, found" has worked incredibly.

Honestly everything worked from the mastermind 😊...including the concept of focusing on the high ticket niches (like roofing vs pest control). Frankie Fihn You were damn right about finding the 1% we can help.

Instead of going after the 99% of roofaz, the magic has been finding the 1% who are entrepreneurs who get it, and all I have to do is give them a tiny push to the finish line instead of building a redneck's biz from the ground up. The guys who have 3 offices and 1 mill marketing budgets already.

The heck with 7 figures, let's hit 8 😄😄😄!!!!

Love · Reply · 2h · Edited

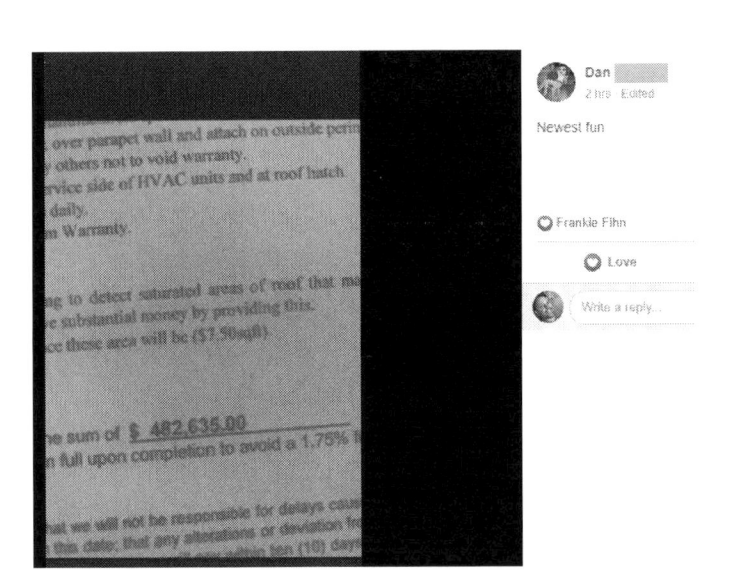

Dan
2 hrs · Edited

Newest fun

○ Frankie Fihn
○ Love

Write a reply...

excerpt of document showing:
over parapet wall and attach on outside perim
others not to void warranty.
vice side of HVAC units and at roof hatch.
daily.
Warranty.

g to detect saturated areas of roof that ma
substantial money by providing this.
these area will be ($1.50sqft).

e sum of $ 482,635.00
full upon completion to avoid a 1.75% f

at we will not be responsible for delays cau
this date, that any alterations or deviation fo
within ten (10) day

> Dude. This man shows up in a McLaren. Sits down with me and pulls out his Gucci bag with $10k rolled up and tells me, I came here to spend money. How much is this going to cost me? Hes got 7 offices but equally he also needs someone to manage the marketing to take it nationally - so going to take equity of his company just focusing on marketing growth

> One of the first commercial leads we got is going to be close to 1 mill

> Meeting is tmw. Profit would be close to 400k. On that deal I only make 3% 😒😊

> The universe is crazy am I right??

Leah Signs Four $12k Clients In A Row

Leah
August 3, 2017 · Add Topics

Signed another private 6-month client in 1.25 calls. That's a 100% close rate (4on4).

You, Michael Barnes, Dan Crystal and 1 other   6 Comments Seen by 3

Love   Comment

Frankie Fihn Put that shit right here home girl...
http://i.imgur.com/b3o7IpE.gif

Like · Reply · 1y

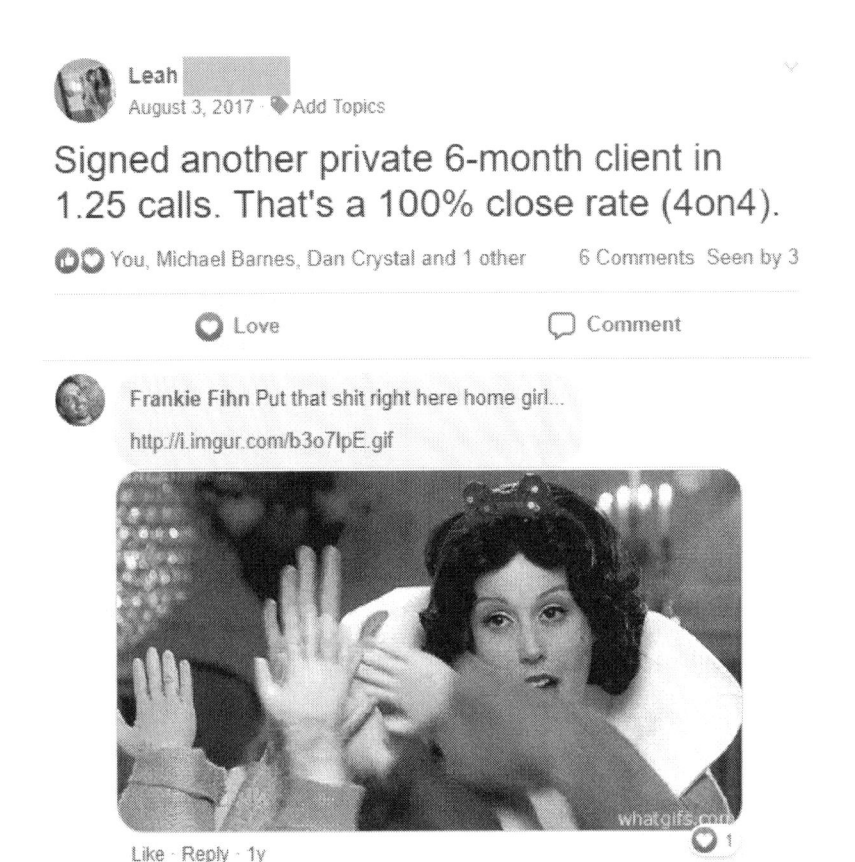

Sandy Picks Up $3k In An Hour

Sandy
30 mins

Big thanks to Frankie Fihn who offered to listen to a call recording and gave me advice on how to improve. I received his input about 15 minutes before a sales call, and was able to make a few significant improvements to my framework. I now have a new $3k client!

Like   Comment

You, Mike Lamothe, Nicola Snoad and 5 others

Frankie Fihn Dude! Go you! 😊 ❤️ 😊
http://i.imgur.com/Azto4Vi.jpg

INTERNET BRO FIST

PLACE FIST HERE

IMGUR.COM

Kate Has Her First $25k Week

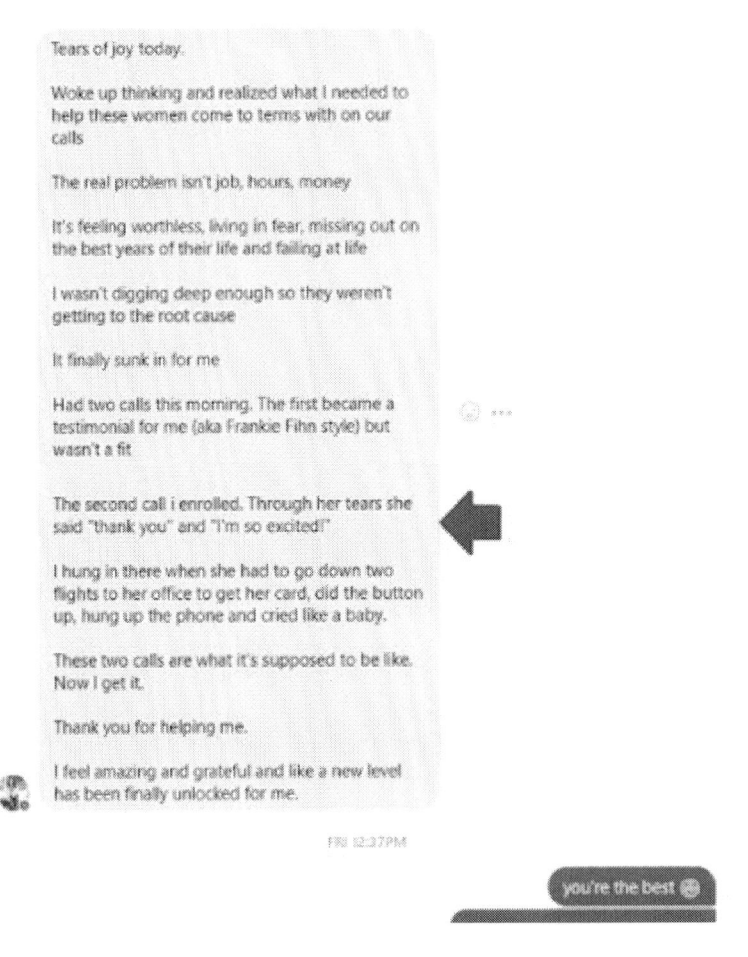

> Tears of joy today.
>
> Woke up thinking and realized what I needed to help these women come to terms with on our calls
>
> The real problem isn't job, hours, money
>
> It's feeling worthless, living in fear, missing out on the best years of their life and failing at life
>
> I wasn't digging deep enough so they weren't getting to the root cause
>
> It finally sunk in for me
>
> Had two calls this morning. The first became a testimonial for me (aka Frankie Fihn style) but wasn't a fit
>
> The second call i enrolled. Through her tears she said "thank you" and "I'm so excited!"
>
> I hung in there when she had to go down two flights to her office to get her card, did the button up, hung up the phone and cried like a baby.
>
> These two calls are what it's supposed to be like. Now I get it.
>
> Thank you for helping me.
>
> I feel amazing and grateful and like a new level has been finally unlocked for me.
>
> FRI 12:37PM

you're the best 😊

Thomas Signs Two $100k Recurring Clients

> **Thomas ▇▇▇** Wanted a refresher on this..... Listen to this shit again, my people!
>
> We've closed two reoccurring clients that add $100K yearly to our bottom line. Note: REOCCURRING.... See More
>
> Like · Reply · 3d · Edited
>
>> **Frankie Fihn** If a degenerate like ▇▇▇ can do it, anyone can.
>>
>> Nice job brother.
>>
>> We'll all celebrate your accomplishment with a dancing banana...
>>
>> https://media.giphy.com/media/IB9foBA4PVkKA/giphy.gif

Reminder: If you're not yet in the free Facebook group Beyond Agency Profits, get your booty in there. It won't be the same without your fine ass inside. I swear that's not as dirty as it sounds. You'll discover a way for getting a new lifetime client every week without Facebook ads, SEO, webinars, or complicated funnels. I love to share it with you for free.

A Small Disclaimer

Of course, I'm not "promising" you these same results. You're a unique human being with your own skill set. I just want to show you what's possible when you apply the power of these timeless principles.

Now here's something else that will save you untold amounts of client headaches.

First Dates Vs Instant Marriage

Imagine for a second you are a man who would like to meet his future wife. You cruise around some night clubs looking for Mrs. Right. You see a pretty stranger and you ask her to get married to you. You keep doing this to stranger after stranger. What do you think will happen?

Probably a whole lot of nos. Perhaps a few laughs, maybe even a drink to the face. Why? Because it's asking too much too soon.

It goes against the normal psychology of how humans form bonds and relationships. The normal process involves first getting to know someone, going out on a few dates, and continuing forward only if it's a fit. Even if you get a yes, what happens when it's totally the wrong fit? What happens when you end up married to a nightmare partner?

Human psychology is the same everywhere. Running an agency is no different. Above all, you are still working with people and building relationships.

Most agencies offer "marriage" right out of the gate. "Pay me thousands every month and I'll generate some leads during that time." You commit to the relationship long term before even knowing if it's a fit for everyone involved. That's instant marriage. It backfires more often than not.

What happens if that client is a huge pain in the ass? What happens if it turns out a client is a lot harder to generate results for than you originally thought? What about that it's really hard to sell marriage? Most times, you just grin and bear it. You're stuck. They're stuck. You're in a crappy marriage together. Divorces are ugly.

A better way is to work together as a "first date". It's a small commitment to feel each other out. That way you get to see if it's a fit for everybody involved.

It's way easier to back out of a first date that didn't go as planned. This protects you from getting married to the wrong clients. The wrong clients will suck the life out of you. It is the single biggest drain you will ever experience.

Plus, a first date makes your client acquisition job easier. First dates are a lot easier to sell. What do you think is an easier yes - pay me thousands of dollars for 12 months or why don't we run a campaign for 7 days and if there are enough results we can talk about the next steps?

A powerful offer and a first date work together. You get to control your fate. When you feel out your clients first, something powerful happens. You become the selector instead of the selected.

Becoming The Hunted Instead Of The Hunter

An agency without control creates slavery. Most freelancers and digital agency owners have money or time but not both together. For them, it is an either or proposition. When they have money, they have no time to enjoy it. When they have time, they are usually broke or severely underpaid.

When you are the selector, you get to have money and time together. You want to build an agency that not only helps your clients but also gives you the kind of lifestyle you've dreamed about. Your impact, results, and leadership will uplevel dramatically. You work less as you earn more.

Chapter 7: An Automated Sales Machine Without The Phone

It's time for you to make some magic happen. This chapter will help you design your entire business with leverage in mind. You will sign clients without the need for being on the phone.

Remember that once your offer is desirable and sexy, there are a lot of ways to get clients. A great offer doesn't need all the arm twisting, persuasion, and coercion that most people rely on.

Having said that, where should you put your offer out there? You don't need to reinvent the wheel. Here are some shortcuts to consistently and repeatedly attract clients with ease and grace.

I have included only the methods that have personally worked for us and our clients. These are the five most successful ways we've used to attract clients.

Strategy #1 - Customized Outreach

If you're broke, this strategy is a lifesaver. Why? Because it works fast and it requires no cash up front. It just takes a little elbow grease and some intelligent hard work. You don't need any cash to get started. You just need a laptop. You can usually get your first client within a day or two. It's ideal if you're just beginning and don't yet have an ad budget to make things happen.

Before you begin, you will need to be able to record your screen while you talk. The software I recommend is called Loom. You can also use Jing or Camtasia. They allow you to record your screen while you talk.

Here's what you do. You go to Google search. You search for the types of clients you would be interested in working with. If you want plumbers, search plumbers. If you want consultants, search consultants. There are mountains of them at the click of a button.

Next you open up their website. Ideally, go to the page with the owner's picture.

Before you begin, what could they do to improve their results? You probably notice a few things that they are doing poorly on their website. That's the easy part. If you are working with offline businesses, this is unbelievably easy. Even with more advanced marketers, there is always something that can be improved.

You hit 'record'. When the video begins, the first thing they see is themselves and their own website. They care a great deal about those things.

You start talking about where they are losing money and a few things you would do to improve their marketing. Most websites are very bad. It shouldn't take you more than 5 seconds to find a few possible improvements. You just share those openly and freely.

If you don't know what to say, there are a few common mistakes almost all businesses are making. They have no social proof. They don't have a clear and powerful offer. Their call to action isn't there. The site loads slowly. You can barely read the phone number. It sounds exactly like their competitor. Their logo takes up half the page. They were hard to find in search. They don't have any reviews on Google. The reviews they have are bad. Their ad is terrible. The language is confusing. You get the idea.

Then when you're finished, you send them a recording. It has a little message that just says, "I noticed a few problems on your website. It was easier to explain in this 5 minute video."

This is known as "cold outreach". Contrary to popular opinion, cold outreach works, especially when it is customized and relevant. The biggest reason cold outreach doesn't work for people is because people copy and paste the same generic message to everyone. We receive the "We are blah blah blah SEO company" message verbatim 100x per week. You could switch the company names and the message is identical. It has no value to anyone.

People don't care about you. They care about themselves and their own business. If you start the conversation with them and their business, they are always interested in hearing what you have to say.

Also you're leading with value and improvements out of the gate. This does something powerful. It demonstrates your expertise. It demonstrates how you can help them with their own blind spots. Demonstrations are infinitely more powerful than a generic message that says "we do Google ads".

Just how powerful are demonstrations? There was a nationwide window company that sold hurricane-proof windows. At one of their conferences, they asked the top salesperson how he sold so many windows.

He was outselling everyone else by orders of magnitude. Second place was miles behind him. A funny thing happened. They were expecting the superman 123 closing technique or the 5 step reverse question mojo. Instead, he just said, "Here's what I do."

He took one of their hurricane-proof windows. He took out a hammer. Without any warning, he thunderously smashed down the hammer on the window. When the window didn't shatter into a million tiny pieces, he said, "See? Hurricane proof windows."

Demonstrations work. I have clients who have been with me over 10 years from this video strategy.

Once you demonstrate your authority, it's just a matter of closing. How do you end the video? You can very gently offer a conversation. "Of course, these aren't the only ideas I have for you. Would it make sense for us to have a conversation to see how I might help? Here's how you can reach me." No fancy sales technique needed.

Typically for every 10 videos you make, you're going to land at least one paying client.

It's time consuming. For that reason, this strategy is not "scalable". When you're doing high 6 figures or 7 figures, you probably don't want to do this anymore.

However, if you're in a situation where your rent is due Friday and it's Wednesday morning, this can get you out of a jam. When you have better cash flow, use your leverage to do the heavy lifting for you. For now, give some customized demonstrations and get some cash in the bank.

Strategy #2 - Case Studies

Once you have some successful clients, turn them into "case studies". Testimonials are somewhat effective. Case studies are testimonials on steroids. They work like gangbusters.

What's the difference? A case study is a client result that you turn into a teaching example. By teaching, it sounds far, far less self-serving.

How does a good case study work? You show the problem the client had, what you tried, what worked, the lessons you learned, and what the ultimate result was. Inevitably, somebody reading it will be in a similar situation and say "I want that result too".

A great case study is far more powerful than saying "We do backlinks" or "we do Google Adwords". If you can build your funnel around just one thing, build it around case studies. Lead those case studies into your offer.

What's the best format for a case study? I haven't found a bad one yet. Case studies have worked for us in organic social marketing. They have worked as a video. They have also worked as part of an email follow up sequence. It works because people are still people in text, video, or any social media platform. What works one place will work just about anywhere. Because other people with that same problem will want your solution.

Strategy #3 - White Label Strategic Partnerships

You can build an entire business just around strategic partnerships. From 2007 to 2011, this is all our agency did.

Our first 100+ SEO and Google Adwords clients came entirely from white label partnerships. The best part was that we never even had to do a single sales call. Our partners sold our services for us!

Our primary partnerships were with web designers. It was a very harmonious relationship because they just wanted to make websites. They got to do what they were good at. They didn't want to do SEO or Adwords. Selling our SEO services gave them another way to monetize their clients. We offered them a $200-500/month discount so they could mark up our services.

Of course, we made the web designers look good too.

It also meant we could sign clients without doing even 5 minutes of "selling". My clients would go out and sell their clients on a web design and SEO package. They white labelled our services.

From a delivery point of view, this meant we slapped their logo on the monthly reports before we sent them out. We also gave their clients a direct number they could call with SEO questions. It was almost no extra work for them. You want to make it as seamless as possible for them.

Who are the complimentary pieces for you? If you do Facebook ads, who sets up their fan page? Who runs their other social media? What about people who run Google ads? Who are the people that help them set up the rest of their funnel or their pages? Who already has your client?

If you do SEO, where are the web designers who don't do SEO? If you do Google ads, who are the people that help them build landing pages? Who are the people that have your client already and don't compete with you?

The answer to these questions are all potential partnerships for you. Work with the people who already have functioning and thriving businesses. You will almost always have to "prove yourself" on a small scale before they give you a bigger piece of the pie. Expect that.

Here's the cool part. All of these people are really easy and open to talk to you. They're already looking for extra ways to monetize.

Strategy #4 - Webinars

I did an interview with a guy who brought in $10,000,000 in sales last year with one webinar. That's not his only one.

He's literally critiqued thousands of webinars; the whole spectrum from extreme successes to sucky losers. He's also helped transform many beasts into beauties.

I asked him 3 very, very interesting questions.

Question 1: "What's the #1 mistake that most people make in a webinar?"

Without hesitation, "They try and teach too many things at once. A confused mind says no."

Question 2: "What's been the most important common thread among your big successes?"

Without hesitation, "It's the offer. A webinar is just a carefully crafted vehicle to deliver a killer offer."

Question 3: "How does one make such a killer offer?" He says most people really just want to know 3 things:

1. "Will it work for me?"
2. "How long is it going to take?"
3. "What can I expect when it's done?"

Powerful stuff that I thought I'd share.

My most successful months (financially speaking) were created through webinars. Though success isn't only determined by monthly revenue. From just one great webinar, we've had our calendars full of new sales leads for months on end. All the people were pre-sold from our webinar. It's not difficult to hit $50k or $100k per month and beyond when they are lining up to work with you.

Just beware that there's a lot more competition with webinars today. There are an abundance of low value "5 steps to blah blah webinars". Your webinar hook needs to stand out from the noise.

Remember funnels are just different vehicles to deliver an offer. Get the offer right before you strap a webinar to it.

Strategy #5 Speaking On Stage

Another strategy that works is speaking on stage. Speaking comes with a certain built in authority.

If you enjoy the adrenaline rush of having an audience, you should speak. Personally, crowds light me up. For some people, it will only make you a nervous wreck. If an audience freaks you out, there are plenty of other introvert-friendly ways to get clients.

If you've never been booked to speak before, here's what I've found works best. You can find a list of associations in your industry. Reach out to them. Offer a unique angle for their next event.

Just like anything else, it's your offer that matters. Have something worthwhile to say to their audience. They are always looking for something new and fresh to give to their audience. If you can make them look good, they will book you.

Whether you get paid directly or not is irrelevant. Because it's the sales that come out of speaking that matter. I have had unpaid speaking gigs. A day later someone would call our agency and say, "We want to buy whatever you have for sale."

Typically you are not allowed to "pitch" at a speaking event. This meant people would go home and Google us later. They didn't even know what our offer was. They just knew they wanted it. It doesn't get any easier than clients served to you on a silver platter.

Take a look at what everyone else is saying at the conferences in your industry. What's something unique and new you could add to that?

If you want to get proven offer templates and messages for your agency, head on over to beyondagencyprofits.com. Grab yours free.

The Instant Authority Hack

When I started my Facebook ad agency for lawyers, no one knew who I was. I had zero connections. I had zero ad budget to reach anyone. I had no "funnels" or "webinars" or anything really.

Not one soul was interested in what we did or what we had to say. I was as unknown as could be.

In 6 months time, I was speaking on the biggest and most prominent stages in our industry.

This helped me land a who's who list of A+ clients. I had many clients who were the cheesy lawyers you see on every billboard across the state.

Here's the thing about becoming an authority that most people don't know. It can be hacked!

Plus, it makes your life a lot easier for your agency. This is because the top clients want the best. People who want the best spend more money with you, give you far less headaches, and stay for a long, long time. Of course, treat them well.

Here's an instant authority hack for your agency to dramatically upgrade your industry status. Collaborate with the top person in your niche. How?

There are a few ways it can be done. My favorite way is to do a simple interview. In the lawyer market, I just called up the top law firm in the USA. I said, "Hey I love what you're doing and I'd love to interview you and share your message."

At the time, I had zero following, knew no one, and didn't have a podcast or anything like that. Without hesitation they said "yes" and offered a few dates that worked. Why?

Because people love talking about themselves. A few weeks later we did our first interview and became friends. I had to be persistent and it probably took at least 18 follow ups. I got rescheduled at least 4 times. Had he said "no", I would have reached out to number 2 on the list.

Just look at the instant credibility it created. Which of these do you think got clients to see me an authority?

Without any existing credibility: "Here are the top 3 ways to get more legal clients."

With the credibility of the top lawyer in the world: "Just yesterday I was talking to John Morgan of Morgan And Morgan, doing over $500,000,000 annually. They are the single biggest law firm in the country with almost 30 locations spanning across the entire Southeastern United States. They spend over $25 million on TV ads alone. Here's what John Morgan told me are the top 3 ways to get more clients."

In both cases, it is the same offer. In the second example, it's just done with a lot more authority. When you make the second statement, guess what happens? Ears perk up.

There is a subtle embedded idea that says, "This guy works with the best so he must also be one of the best." So here's the deal. If you don't have authority, you can borrow it.

You can borrow it in a big way. One thing I've learned from my many ayahuasca experiences is that the purpose of business is to make our customer's lives better. If you can actually change people's lives, you owe it to yourself. Put yourself out there with authority. Borrowing authority might just help you get there a lot faster.

Now let's get back to getting yourself off the phone and free. This is all about working on the right things and understanding the big picture.

Leverage Is Your Key To Freedom!

When it comes to getting things done, you are always operating from one of 4 levels.

- **Level 1: The Firefighter**

This is when you're working on what's

seemingly urgent and pressing. You are very reactionary to email and text messages. If a client emails you and asks you to call them, you dial them up as soon as humanly possible. If you get an email, you feel the need to respond to it immediately. Most of your day is spent reacting.

- **Level 2: The Prioritizer**

This is where you're not responding to the urgent messages. Instead you're working on what's most important. Sometimes what's urgent and what's important are the same. However, most times they aren't. You are more proactive in this stage than in level 1. You have learned that it's okay for people to wait a little while.

- **Level 3: The Long Term Thinker**

This is where you're *not* just thinking about what's important now. You're also thinking about the long term potential. You are playing the long game and the short game at the same time. You're working on what's most important and what has the ability to keep paying you again and again over time. You prioritize projects that create leverage for you.

If a project can pay you $10,000 today and $10,000 every year, that is more valuable than just making a single $10,000 sale today. You are building things that have both a short term and long term pay off.

- **Level 4: The Automated Asset Machine**

This is similar to level 3. It is working on important projects for the short and long term value. What's different now is that you are creating processes and systems. You are systematizing asset creation that pays you over time. Your people, systems, and processes create assets automatically. Just like Ray Kroc doesn't have to make every Big Mac or open every new store. His processes do most of the heavy lifting. You are focused on removing yourself from the equation so you don't have to be the one creating everything. Your processes and systems clone your abilities. You get your way done and other people do it for you.

Most freelancers and agency owners spend their time on level 1. It's the least productive work there is. Being a long term asset creator is where you're going to find your freedom. Choose to be in the higher levels more often.

Get On The Phone To Get Off The Phone

There is a very important milestone you must achieve to have a freedom-based agency. You must get off the phone. Your sales process needs to convert without the phone calls. In order to do that, you actually *do* want to get on the phone first. However, you use the phone with a very specific purpose in mind.

Before that though, you must sell your services on the phone ethically. Ethical selling is a beautiful thing. It means more than anything, you don't over promise just to get a credit card. You're actually helping people and only offering what you can actually deliver.

Begin with the right intention in mind. You can leverage your sales and scale without spending all day on the phone.

How To Automate And Leverage Your Sales

Here's the process for getting off the phone. For example, I used to do a lot of phone calls with lawyers. After a hundred phone calls, you hear the same things again and again. It becomes like a broken record. The same questions and problems repeat. Here's an example.

Lawyer: "I need more clients."

Me: "Why do you need more clients?"

Lawyer: "I have rollercoaster income."

Me: "What do you mean?"

Lawyer: "I don't really have any control over my business. One month I will make $2,000 and the next month $40,000. I never know if I can pay my bills or not. I am very stressed out."

Me: "Why does that happen?"

Lawyer: "I'm dependent on referrals. I never know what my referral partners are going to send me each month. Some months it is a lot. Other months they don't have anything. I don't have any control over them."

Words Of Pure Gold

You have extreme power when you can see their core issue with great clarity. Why? Because that's what goes right back into your marketing.

Imagine you're a lawyer and you get an email like this one. "Do you have rollercoaster income? Does that mean you don't know whether you're going to pay your bills or scale? Are your ups and downs because you have no control over your referrals? Do your partners send you 6 referrals one month and zero the next? Joe was able to eliminate them in his practice. Here's a case study on how he did it."

Therein lies your purpose for the phone. You want to get deep insight. You want to know their problem better than they do. Doing this enables you to speak to them on a deep, deep level. This handles their biggest objection right away.

Stay on the phone until you know their problem in specific detail. When it comes to creating powerful marketing, pros don't guess. You cannot speak to clients unless you truly know what's happening in their reality.

You are only getting on the phone so you hit the bullseye. Once you have their exact problem in their exact words, you have the leverage you need. You can speak to that problem through email, through retargeting ads or anything else automated and leverageable.

It is powerful because it is deeply insightful.

When you put that kind of leverage into your marketing, the phone calls quickly become unnecessary. When you have a "sales" call, it will be 5 minutes long. "Hey I just have a quick question." Nine times out of ten, that question will be, "Will this work for my situation?"

Having Only Pre-Sold Clients

Once you understand their real problem in their own words and the nuances of it, you don't need the phone again. You also don't have to convince anyone. They're already convinced. They've lived with the problem long enough to know it needs fixed.

The whole "sales call" is unnecessary or extremely brief when you have already addressed everything beforehand. You've already done the "convincing" before a call is necessary.

You are mostly going to get, "Will this work for me?" By then, you can also close in chat or by email. Closing is a matter of a simple, "Can you tell me a little bit about your situation?" Followed by a simple "yes we can help" or "no we cannot". The phone is not needed to do that.

Before you get on the phone, have a plan. Get out a pen and paper and take good notes. Record the call if you can. Get their exact wording word for word.

You want to think about using the phone as a leverageable asset. Put that into marketing. Why do you want to have that conversation in your marketing instead of in a sales call? Here's why:

Marketing Is Leverageable. Sales Are Not.

You cannot leverage "sales". It is a very difficult process. That's why sales managers get paid big salaries and have to train and motivate their staff daily.

Most people rely on their sales to do the heavy lifting. They get on the phone with people who are mostly 3 out of 10 sold on working with them. They are long ways away from being "sold". They use the sales call to bridge that gap.

By using your marketing to accomplish this, you will only deal with people who are 8 out 10 or better about working with you. It makes the sales call far less important. It also makes it far more repeatable.

If you have 5 blog posts that do the heavy lifting for you, that is leverageable. If you have a great webinar that presells, that is leverageable. If you have a case study video that converts, that is leverageable. You want your marketing to do your selling, not your phone persuasion skills.

There is another reason to do it this way. It reduces refunds dramatically. This is because clients sell themselves on you. If you need to "persuade" people on a phone call, they often regret it later. Don't be surprised when they act wishy washy after the sale.

You want your marketing on point so every single person on the phone with you is pre-sold and prequalified.

Once your marketing is there, the phone is unnecessary. They are already "sold" long before that point. That gives you massive leverage to scale and grow. It also allows you to actually be free. Plus how hard is it to find good sales people when they aren't coercing anyone? It's dog shit simple because your leads already know they want to work with your company.

Now, let's take a short detour. If you still do traditional lead generation, here are a few shortcuts. You can use these to get your clients results faster. They have been battle tested through years of experience.

A Couple Random Hacks That Accelerate Your Lead Generation Results

SEO Results:

Firstly, understand that Google is mostly full of shit. Ignore everything Google tells you to do. "Hey just make quality content and people will link to you automatically." You've probably heard that bullshit before. Only follow that strategy if you want to never rank or make any money. Otherwise, here's a better path.

Always reverse engineer rankings and see *what's working in Google now*. Because actions speak louder than words. You'll learn far more from observing Google's actions than trying to follow what Google is saying. Listen to Google's behavior, not their words. Find number one sites and look at their link profile. See what they have done. Do what the top sites do. You will learn the most by seeing what makes the number one sites number one.

Paid Ad Results:

Pros do not guess with their message. They know with absolute certainty what their market needs and wants. Connect to your audience. Spend some time beforehand in either a Facebook group or a discussion forum. Read your potential customers comments, questions, and concerns.

You want to pay extra close attention to comments and discussions with a lot of upvotes and a lot of activity. That's where the gold is. Often you can use those posts word for word as ads.

The most important part of writing successful ads is knowing what people want before you begin. Great ad writing starts before a single word has been written. It starts with understanding the person you are writing to.

Your ads will come across as deeply and insightful. That's because they are.

You did what no one else did. You listened.

Chapter 8: *Scratches Ears* Good Boy! Training Your Clients To Behave

You will only ever have four types of clients.

1. Low paying - High maintenance clients
2. Low paying - Low maintenance clients
3. High paying - High maintenance clients
4. High paying - Low maintenance clients

All of your clients will fall into one of these four categories. Life gets easier when you choose clients who fall into category 4. What happens if you have bad clients right now? What happens to clients who are low paying and high maintenance?

Fire Them! Yes You Can Fire Clients!

Want to eliminate 90% of the headaches in your agency? Fire your low paying high maintenance clients immediately. If you think you need their cash, you don't. The loss of revenue is usually minor. However, the gain you will experience in sanity is astronomical. They are a drain on energy and time, which are far more valuable than the little bit of money they pay you.

I remember my worst clients. One of them talked down to my staff. She demanded $40,000 worth of work for less than $1000. She wanted miracles daily. She demanded frequent meetings and phone calls, usually everyday. If we took 2 hours to respond to an email, she bitched at how that was unacceptable. She didn't answer her phone and then blamed us for bad leads. It's hard to articulate just how condescending every interaction was.

So we fired her! It was one of the freest moments in my agency. My assistant Terence actually did a little celebration dance. We gave them a refund and moved on.

Another bad client put a 12 minute voice greeting between our leads and working with him. If I mailed him a $100,000 check, he was the kind of person who wouldn't have walked to the mailbox to pick it up. Of course, he blamed us. Bad clients usually blame you for things they do themselves. Our leads hung up because they had to wait 12 minutes and push 7 button combinations to get through to a human. Often their system would disconnect you after you waited that whole time.

You just don't need people like that in your agency. Be willing to let go of any client who is more headaches than they are worth.

The Secret Weapon That Eliminates 90% Of Client Problems Before They Happen

Do you find that the hardest part of running your agency is by far the clients themselves? Take some good notes. Because this next section will make your life exponentially easier.

Why do bad clients happen? What causes them in the first place? What is the source of all those headaches, frustrations, and problems? More importantly, what is the one thing that makes them go away before they even happen?

It's not what most people think it is. Most people think it's getting better results for your clients. It's not that.

A good friend owns the biggest ad agency in Europe. He spent $100,000 hiring the best ad team in the world to get better client results.

They achieved it. They got better client results. He still had the same client complaints 3 months later.

Because it's not about *results*. It's about *expectations*. What results were they expecting?

Setting Expectations So Everyone Wins

You want to be a master of setting proper, realistic expectations. For example, I remember my friend saying, "It's like I have 160 different bosses." He kept investing heavily in making his team better. He worked harder and harder to get better client results. He kept getting them more leads, scaling better, and lowering their ad costs. Still he had the same complaints!

His best client result went from $10k/month to $400k/month in just 90 days. Then that client did the unthinkable. They fired him. Nothing says "thank you" to an extra $390k per month quite like a pink slip.

The other clients getting lesser results were still mostly unhappy. He couldn't seem to please anyone. They wanted meetings, explanations, text messages, email responses, etc etc.

It wasn't until he realized that the big underlying problem was actually the client expectations. If you set your client's expectations right from the very beginning, it builds trust. Trust is what makes your job easy. A client who trusts you just lets you do your thing. Everything goes much smoother with trust. Trust comes through a foundation of proper expectations.

Setting Expectations Like A Boss

Hopefully you understand just how important expectations really are. Now, how do you set them properly so everyone wins? How do you do it effectively so it leads to happy, patient, grateful clients?

The Four Key Areas Of Expectations.

1. **Results:** What results are you going to get them? How is that success measured?

2. **Time:** How long is it going to take?

3. **Cost:** How much money do they have to spend?

4. **Communication**: What are you going to communicate and how often?

All problems of expectation happen in one or more of these areas. Happy relationships happen when you're on the same page in these 4 areas.

When you specify all 4 of these variables in advance, clients get you. They understand your work. Your clients actually understand what you're doing for them. That's when the trust flows.

Specificity = Patient, Happy, Grateful Clients

Here's the key. You must be specific. The clearer and more concise expectations you set in those 4 areas, the easier your life gets.

Specificity makes your clients easier to deal with. In our line of work, the vast majority of client headaches happen because you and your client weren't on the same page. They are almost always problems of expectations in disguise.

What You Thought vs What Your Client Thought

Imagine this scenario and compare these two totally different points of view.

A new accountant client hires you for Facebook ad services. You're stoked to see a new payment in your Stripe account. You ask for their website logins and get access to their ad accounts. After a little back and forth, you've set up all the necessary pixels and tracking codes.

They've hired someone to run other ads before but never on Facebook before. They liked Google but thought it was too expensive. They're excited at the idea of getting cheap clients.

You are starting your ad journey from absolute zero. The client has no working funnel, their website is old and frankly pretty shitty, and their messaging sounds like every other accountant in the area.

First, you come up with an idea for a good lead magnet. Since this offer has never been tested before, you hope you can get $8 leads. With leads that cheap, you figure everybody will be really happy.

You set up your first test ad and target other local business owners in the area. Much to your surprise, the ad starts bringing $4 to his email list right away. This is a huge success! You are already getting results out of the gate.

Two more weeks go by and you get an email from your client. They sound frazzled. "I just got a $500 bill from Facebook on my Visa and I still don't have a single paying client. Can you call me right away? Can we pause our ads?"

Of course this scenario is just an example. However, it happens every day in the real world. Where did it all go wrong?

- **What you thought:** My client hired me to get cheap leads. I helped them get $4 leads right away. I am doing a great job.

- **What your client thinks:** I believe ads are binary. They either work or they don't. I don't see what running them longer would do if they aren't working now. I don't understand refining and testing. All I know is I got a $500 bill and I still don't have a single client. The ads are not working. I knew I should not have trusted another ad person. I didn't even receive a single phone call. You are spending my hard earned money. I didn't want "leads". I wanted clients!

Here's the thing though. It's not because the ads didn't work. It's because the expectations were off course. Remember, these are 4 key areas of expectations.

1. Results
2. Time

3. Cost
4. Communication

Unfortunately for you, you missed the mark on all of them. Even the cheap leads you got, 'cheap' is relative to what you expected. They've never ran Facebook ads before. They don't know what's a good or bad lead cost. They're not "cheap" to him, especially if he doesn't yet have a client to show for it.

What should you have done differently? Imagine before you ran a single ad, you sent your new client a one page pdf document. The goal was to get everyone on the same page. Before you hit go, they signed off on it. The document said something like this.

What You Should Expect In Our First 30 Days Of Working Together.

Results: You have never run ads before on Facebook. This means we are beginning this process without a working offer or funnel. We are starting from absolute zero. A big win in month one would be to get leads for under $10. We will be testing a lot of angles. We are finding out what your customers respond to. We are trying approaches so your message stands out from all of your competitors. There is no "magic button". Our ads will probably not magically land you a client on day 1. However, this is a normal part of the process. We will continue to nurture every lead we get. Remember that many leads we get today will convert into phone calls 3-12 months down the road. It may not look like "immediate sales" but this is tremendous progress. Please stay patient during this process.

Time: We expect to be able to generate leads for under $10 in the first 10 days. You will see the first leads on the first day we run ads.

Cost: We will be spending up to $1000 this month. This means you will probably get a bill from Facebook after the first $25. They often bill in increments of a few $100. Don't be alarmed when you see this charge on your credit card. We are investing your money today to sure up future business tomorrow. Remember that $10 is a small price to pay for someone who could become a $10,000 or more client for you.

Communication: We will send you a full report at the end of the month. It will show you the leads and what we paid. We will also explain what we tested and why. We typically do not do phone meetings. Time on the phone could have been better used to improve your results. If you have any questions, you can text me or email. We typically respond within 48 hours.

Can you please sign off below that you read this? I want to be 100% sure we are on the same page.

By the way, if you're still making proposals, these are the same 4 things you want to talk about.

When Should You Calibrate Expectations?

The best time is before you begin. Even before a client gets their first bill, their first report, or their first campaign goes live, you should calibrate their expectations. Later it is often too late. Later any explanation sounds more like "backpedaling" and excuse making.

For example, I once got on the phone with a bigshot lawyer who had a phone team of 10. He told me emphatically that they closed almost 100% of the leads they get. "If it's a client we want, we close it almost every time."

In my experience, I knew that to be complete bullshit. Local businesses are generally terrible at phone calls. Lawyers might even be worse than the average. There was virtually no chance he was converting all the phone calls they were getting.

I decided to do a test phone call and record it. I called his office pretending to be someone who hurt their back in an accident. I listened as their team fumbled and bumbled and lost me as a potential lead.

I then sent him an email with the recording. The email said, "Do you still think you convert 100% of your phone calls?" He was a little embarrassed but very open to our help and suggestions.

That's not how most agencies do it. They try to set the expectations after they aren't closing those phone calls like they should.

We could have generated leads for him for 2 or 3 months. At some point, he would have told us they are bad leads and they aren't working for him. At this point, we would probably try to tell him to do a better job closing. When we tell him he is bad at the phone, does he believe us? Or does it sound like backpedaling and explaining?

There is an important lesson in this scenario. It's way easier to get your client on the same page on day 1 than on day 90. Win their trust from the beginning. Set specific expectations in all 4 areas.

It is far easier to deal with problems of expectation before they come up. Set your expectations powerfully up front. You will eliminate more than 90% of the typical client headaches. It will make your agency life a lot easier.

Clients Who Understand The Process Cooperate

Remember the accountant you got $4 leads for? Let's pretend that this time around you set better expectations.

Believe it or not, you could get worse results and he would be happier. You could get $12 leads, take 3 months longer, never once call your client, accidentally blow through $3000 in test ads, and still he would most likely be a happier client. That is the power of setting expectations. A client who knows what to expect trusts you.

How do most freelancers and agencies set expectations? It's only in their head. If what to expect is only in your head, you can never actually keep clients happy.

Of course there is a compound effect. If you have a Beyond Agency, choose the right clients, and properly set expectations, then you will have positively thrilled clients. They end up being your raving fans.

Chapter 9: How To Exceed Expectations And Deliver A Wow Client Experience

Imagine that every client who paid you even one time was still paying you now. Let's also assume they are happy and thrilled. How much more would you be earning now? If you had never lost a single client, what would your monthly income be? Would it create a big snowball effect?

That's because keeping clients is far more valuable than selling new ones. The single most important number in your agency is not how many clients you sign, but how many you keep, upsell, and retain. If you could only pay attention to one key performance indicator in your agency, this is the most important number.

The better the experience you deliver, the easier keeping clients is.

Most Agencies Are Remarkably Average

Most agencies deliver mediocre results. They have average and unremarkable service. They don't do much to show their clients they really value them.

It's not just your competitor agencies either. That's how most businesses operate. When was the last time someone has really impressed you? When was the last time you weren't just another name and number? When was the last time you had a truly remarkable customer experience? It's probably been a while, right? Those experiences are pretty rare.

The Power Of A Remarkable Client Experience

How do you create more than just happy clients? How do you create absolute raving fans who swear by your company and what you do? It's about the client experience you create.

It's important to understand this. Very little of exceeding client expectations has anything to do with the service you offer and what you do. In fact, it has nothing to do with marketing, leads, sales, or even getting results. Don't get me wrong, without results, you certainly won't keep a client. However, it is far deeper than that.

You are going above and beyond the call of duty *intentionally*. Once you understand the key touchpoints in the customer journey, it is simple to create a remarkable customer experience.

Clients Want To Feel Appreciated And Wanted

A wow experience is created by *how you make a client feel*. It is what you do above and beyond the call of duty. They want to feel that their business is appreciated, they are wanted, and that they are valued as a human being.

You should read 'Never Lose A Customer Again' by Joey Coleman and 'Giftology' by John Ruhlin. They both go into these concepts more deeply. The following is a compact analysis on how we applied these principles in our agency. These strategies are timeless. They will work for you as well as for your clients.

The 8 Phases Of Your Client's Journey

Phase 1: They are assessing their situation.

Phase 2: They admit they have a problem and need your help.

Phase 3: They are assessing you and your company as a potential solution.

Phase 4: They are activated as a client.

Phase 5: They become acclimated to your way of doing things.

Phase 6: They accomplish their original goal.

Phase 7: They adopt your principles of business.

Phase 8: They become an advocate of your company.

Now let's be real. Typically, in most agencies most clients don't make it through all these stages. They rarely make it through this entire journey. It happens for many reasons. Mostly it's because the agency drops the ball in one of these critical stages. They are not aware of the client journey. As a result, they fumble and bumble their way through it.

Customer Service vs Department Of Gratitude

How do most agencies handle the client journey? They typically have some kind of "customer service" process. Usually you can contact the owner, the salesperson, or a customer service rep by email and phone number. They do their best to answer client concerns as fast as they can.

The problem with "customer service" is that it is *playing defense*. It is waiting for a problem to arise and then being reactionary.

Your agency is much better served having a "department of gratitude". A department of gratitude is *playing offense*.

Rather than waiting for client problems, you are proactively creating happy client experiences. You don't wait until a client is unhappy. You design your client processes intentionally so client happiness is inevitable. Your process should ensure that happy clients are the only possible outcome.

Wow Experience Shortcuts We Learned

You never get a second to make a first impression. What happens immediately after your client commits to you? Most of the time they will experience some form of "buyer's remorse".

Buyer's remorse is the name for a typical buyer response to a big purchasing decision. This is usually the result of mistakes made in the past and worrying that history may repeat itself. While you did not create their automatic buyer's remorse, it is your job to fix it. It is also your opportunity to wow your new client.

If you could hear your new client's thoughts, it might sound something like this. "What if I just made a mistake? What if I just got ripped off by another smooth-talking salesperson? What will my friends and family think? What if I end up looking stupid and foolish for this decision? What if I just wasted my money?"

This is an automatic human response. Everyone has bought something that didn't turn out the way they thought. Everyone has bought something from a pro salesperson and then the service and delivery underwhelmed them.

That's why the first impression is also a tremendous chance for you to really impress your new client. It is an opportunity to reaffirm that they made the right decision and that they are in good hands with you.

First Impression: Edible Arrangement

One thing we did is order an Edible Arrangement immediately after a client signed. For about $65 including delivery, we sent salted chocolate caramel apples.

Here is a brand new client worried about having made a potential mistake. A few hours later, a delivery man shows up at their door with some delicious salted chocolate dessert and a personalized thank you message. Whatever fears that they were "ripped off" are suddenly put to rest. They feel they are in good hands. They feel great about the decision they just made.

Of course, the experience was by design. That means it was also very systematized and organized. The welcome message was completely standardized except for the client's name. It only took us all of 90 seconds to place an online order to make a great first impression. It was a little work to create a great big effect.

All in all this ran us about $65. Most times they would deliver it within hours on the same day. Sometimes they couldn't receive it until the next morning. It never once failed to make a wow impression.

The First 2 Weeks Together: Signed Picture

I "borrowed" this next idea. I got invited to a mastermind meeting in Las Vegas with 12 of the biggest lawyers in America. Every single one was the biggest in their state. Seeing how they managed their client welcome was inspiring.

We created a standardized welcome package. The top law firms would send a gift basket with a picture of their entire staff. The entire photo would be signed by everyone on the team.

Our welcome package had a few different parts. First, I had our team take a picture with a big blank sign. When we printed the picture, it was signed by everyone on staff. Then we used the magic of Photoshop to put the client's name on the sign. We used a handwritten font so it looked very real. If our client's name was Joe, the sign said, "Welcome Joe". The end result was a photo of the whole team welcoming our client, signed by our entire staff.

Of course, from a delivery point of view, this was all standardized. Everything was prepared in advance. When I learned this from the top law firms, they would hand sign 100 letters at a time. It took each staff member 5 minutes. Then when they got a new client, it only took a minute to get the photo out the door.

It looks like we really all posed together to welcome you personally. It shows a level of care and attention that you just don't see anymore.

If that sounds like a lot of work, it's not. Because it is all prepared in advance. When a new client signs, it's just a matter of taking 5 minutes to photoshop in their name, print out a few documents, and drop it into the mail.

Next in the welcome package was a page restating the expectations. The package also included a letter from me personally. I would state how we intend to do such a good job that they will refer to us business. This letter is called a "Master Referral Letter". It planted the seeds for referrals later.

The package would typically arrive by mail a week or two later.

We did this simultaneously as we ordered the Edible Arrangement. Because of the delay in receiving physical mail, the new client received the Edible Arrangement and welcome package separately. It now seems like two separate moments of exceeding expectation.

From a service and delivery point of view, it's just one single event. For each new client, sending an Edible Arrangement and mailing a welcome package added about 10 minutes of extra work. It cost us less than $70 total. The investment is well worth the total effect it has on our clients. When they are staying years longer, it is because you invested in the relationship from the beginning.

The Middle Lull: Personalized Text Message

After the initial "high" wears off, you will be in the client grind stage. The biggest thing that typically goes wrong here is that they worry you aren't doing anything. Most times you are working on their account and don't have time to message them about it constantly. This is the stage where you want to "over communicate". The more you can keep your communication proactive and intentional the better the client will feel.

We used an automated follow up text messaging to contact clients at weeks 4, 6, 8, 12, and 16. It works very similar to an autoresponder campaign. The text message seems like I'm reaching out to them personally to see how they are doing.

They don't have to be brilliant messages. Some of our messages are as simple as, "Just working on your ads today and excited for the good things that are happening." What matters most to them is *not* the results. It's the fact that you are seemingly on top of things.

Chances are someone in the past has taken their money and ran. Many others have delivered dismal results. That is the previous experience that was created before you. They don't know you have their situation under control unless you communicate it to them.

When clients don't hear from you, they automatically assume the worst. They think maybe you took their money and ran or you just aren't doing anything. In reality, most times it's a sign of the opposite. You are hard at work on their campaigns. However, they don't know that.

That's why proactive communication goes a long way. This is especially if it is seemingly unplanned and unexpected. Of course, you planned and scheduled them in advance.

Most agencies under-communicate. Their idea of "communication" is to send you a monthly bill and a report. Most normal humans can't even read your reports. They are usually overly technical and confusing. If a confusing report is all a client can judge you on, it creates doubt and distrust in your abilities. In today's busy world, talking like a real human is a powerful way to stand out.

You can automate and leverage all of this. Plan your drip fed communication before you begin. Be ready for the middle lull.

Referral Devices: Free Assessment

If you get your clients some results, at some point they are going to express relief or happiness. This is the exact moment when you want to have the referral conversation. A referral device comes in handy to make this seamless and easy. Referral clients cost nothing to acquire, they are pre-sold before they work with you, and they typically spend more than other types of clients.

Our referral device was effective and simple. We created 3 business cards. Each card said something like, "This VIP card entitles you to one free assessment of your website and ads ($500). With this free assessment, most times we can save you or make you at least $1000. There is no obligation. It is just our special way of saying thanks."

How does a referral device work? In order for someone to introduce you to their friends, family, and colleagues, you have to make their job easy. You have to make introducing your business an easy conversation. Don't rely on their ability to brag about you.

Don't "ask" for referrals. That's just begging for business in disguise. Referrals work best when you can make your client look like a hero. Give them something of value. Give them something they can give away that makes them look good. What 'value add' can you give your clients to make referring you easy? Your best clients will refer you to more business.

The 6 Media To Create Client Experiences

Instead of just copying what we do, why not create your own wow customer experience? Here are all the ways you can add value.

1. In-person
2. Email
3. Mail
4. Phone
5. Video
6. Gift

In each of the 8 steps of the customer journey, you can use these 6 media. Every above and beyond touch adds to your overall wow experience. Even if you can't implement them all in one day, just 1 extra touch is more than 99.9% of your competitors will ever do. Multiple touches create a sense of truly caring. You are creating a strategically designed wow experience from start to finish.

Personalized Client Presents Show You Care

The average agency loses their clients in less than 3-6 months. If you are serious about building a real agency that is based on retaining clients, gifts are a powerful strategic tool; especially a personalized gift that hits the bullseye. There is never a bad time for a *meaningful* client gift.

In general, you want to invest 5-10% of what you earn to keep a client. If a client is paying you $2500/month then $100-250 is a small price to pay to retain that client for years longer.

This is why your department of gratitude is so important. They will make retention almost automatic.

You need to know who your clients really are as people. The good news is that social media has made this really easy. Your clients whole lives are up for display. It takes all of 5 minutes for you to scan their public profile. You can see what they really like and don't like.

Here are some things we want to know about each client.

- Family and Pets.
- Affiliations.
- Hobbies.
- Passions.
- Important Experiences.
- Likes/Random Quirks.
- Important/Meaningful Dates.

You may not get every detail. Gather what you can. It's not about filling out your spreadsheet. It's about finding places where you can connect with your clients on a deep personal level.

Of course, don't use your client's information just as marketing. You need to actually care about your clients as people. Take an interest in who they are and what makes them tick. Here are a few examples of how we've used this information.

We Love Our Clients And Their Dogs

One of our clients posted a status update on Facebook. They were sad because they were working so hard and their dogs were mostly home alone. She had 4 beautiful dogs and in the last 2 weeks, they didn't have much attention.

We sent her an industrial size box of doggy treats from Amazon. It had a little note inside. "Dear doggies, this is my make up present."

It was only $12 and it brought a huge smile to her life. We got back the sweetest little video of her feeding her dogs treats. Her face lit up like a Christmas tree.

Gone But Not Forgotten

Another client tragically lost his son to a drug overdose. I got to know his son very well over the years. I still message him on his son's birthday to let them know he still matters. I think it brings them peace to know he is not forgotten.

SWAT Team Hero

Another one watches almost zero television. No Netflix. No movies. Nada. He is a busy entrepreneur. There is just one show he watches and loves called SWAT. He is a big fan of the main character played by Shemar Moore called Hondo. He told me he was remodelling his office. I sent him a custom signed Hondo photo for his office. It was under $30.

The Nature Boo Woo!

Another client grew up in the same town as wrestling legend Ric Flair. He is a huge fan of the Nature Boy himself. Ric Flair is famous for his "woo" taunt. In every single email, we include a "woo" gif. What do you think a client would rather read in an email - a 20 page boring keyword report or their all time favorite wrestler doing his signature chant?

A Personalized Appreciation Note

We also send each client handwritten letters. There are multiple affordable services online to send them for $1.50-$6 each. There is a level of care and attention when you receive a personalized handwritten note in your mailbox. Of course, our notes are both standardized and yet customized.

Again, these are all prepared in advance and drip fed over a time interval. Do you have a detailed plan to wow your clients for the first 180 days? Is it clear what will get done at each step? Are they systematized and organized in advance? Is it set up so you don't even have to think about it?

What Matters To Your Clients?

There are so many ways you can create a wow impression. What are your clients' kids names? What about their pets? What sports teams are they crazy about? Who is their favorite musician? Where did they go to college? What are they passionate about? What experiences are meaningful and significant to them? What are some of their random quirks? What do they like to eat and drink?

Again, you don't need to guess. Anyone can see this information right there in their social media.

For just a few bucks, a virtual assistant on fiverr can gather all the info for you. Even if you are a brand new freelancer, you can do this. Because you don't even have to do it yourself.

Almost no one takes the time to look at this key information. Except you. You're different.

Be clear on how you're going to deliver your wow experience before you even sign your client. Documented processes and procedures separate the amateurs from the professionals. Be a pro.

The Difference Is Exponential

Can you see the difference this creates? Can you imagine what a profound impact it has on a client? Can you imagine how much more enjoyable working with you is compared to another agency?

Your average agency runs a mediocre service, gets mediocre results, never communicates expectations, doesn't understand their own client journey, does nothing extra, and gets fired quickly without any referrals.

They are generally poor communicators and don't know how to do it differently. It's not malicious. They just don't know any better.

A Beyond Agency runs a great service, gets almost immediate results, proactively communicates, understands their client journey, surprises and shows them they are appreciated at every corner, goes above and beyond to appreciate them as people, and makes it very easy for their clients to refer to them.

They are generally proactive communicators and they intentionally choose to be different. They know better.

Chapter 10: "The Thirty Year Wealth Shortcut" – Travis Sago

A special thanks to my mentor and genius Travis Sago for the brilliant ideas that follow. Ready to take a massive financial and freedom leap forward? Because the following principles will redefine everything. It will change what you are creating in your agency.

Most digital marketing agency owners are working towards the wrong end. They are trading time for money. It may look like their own business but in actuality, they just own their own job. They believe they are "providing a service".

Let's dispel that myth right away. Contrary to popular opinion, you are *not* a service provider.

You are an entrepreneur, an investor, and a partner. As an entrepreneur, your time and energy are finite. You cannot get more time. You certainly don't have unlimited energy. You must invest them strategically and wisely.

As long as you trade money for monthly services, your income will have a cap. Eventually you will be too busy to earn more. Not to mention the stress of being constantly rushed.

In a typical agency, more money means you become too busy to enjoy it. Less money means freedom that you are too broke to really utilize. Most people end up with money or freedom but not both together. You can have both together.

Wealth Shortcut #1 - Strategic Asset Acquisition

Have you ever played chess? How about checkers? Chess is a strategic game. Masters train for a lifetime on all the nuances. Checkers can be taught to an 8 year old in under an hour. An amateur chess player will beat a great checkers player every time. A strategic entrepreneur will beat a trading-time-for-dollars freelancer every time.

Why does it matter? Beginner and intermediate agency owners work for money.

Rich People Do Not Work For Money.

Rich people work for assets that generate money. It's a subtle shift that has a huge impact on your bottom line. Assets can be used to generate cash over and over. Rich people especially work for assets that can be created once to keep paying them again and again.

Assets accumulate over time. Cash flow comes and goes.

As a digital marketing expert, what is the one underutilized asset that you should covet the most? The customer list. The money is always in the customer list. Nobody else sees this. The customer list is a powerful leverage point for you to fully understand.

Which of these is more valuable - a $2500 per month contract to do SEO or control of a 2500 person customer list? The answer is the customer list.

Why? Because customers can be sold to again and again for life, provided you treat them well. The $2500 SEO contract might last 12 months if you are lucky. A customer list can pay for you the next 20 years. Given the choice, choose the list.

Yet most freelancers are working only for the money. If you don't have the money you want *today*, it's probably because *yesterday* you were focused on making money instead of acquiring assets. Your money will go in up-and-down cycles. That ends once you have assets working for you. Get your assets to work for you. Stop working only for money.

Here's the cool part. You don't have to choose either or. You can have both! You can actually work for both assets and cash at the same time. It only takes a few slight modifications to your average typical agency.

It requires being more strategic in your thinking and approach. Are you thinking 2-3 steps ahead? Or are you offering monthly lead services for cash? Because to execute this strategy, you will need to be thinking 2 steps ahead.

How do you get someone to just hand over their list of customers to you?

Wealth Shortcut #2 - Trash Can Assets.

I just had a conversation with a roofing company in Southern California with a customer list of 1700 people served over 10 years.

In 10 years, they have never once marketed to their past customers. They never once asked if their customers knew anybody else who needed a roof fixed. They never offered a special deal or gave extra value. They never once offered something complimentary. They never once even bothered to put all those names into a list. Their customer names were literally in 20 boxes of invoices hidden in the back of the office.

That's a "trash can asset". It's an asset that a business wouldn't otherwise be using. It represents zero current value to them. It's underappreciated, undervalued, and underutilized. Of course, it is actually a highly valuable asset. Because they have a relationship with buyers. It's just not being used properly.

That's important for you because that asset is "in the trash can". Because it has no inherent worth to them because they don't understand it.

Trash can assets are easy to control. When we offer, "I think you may have some gold over there in your dumpster. Would it be cool if I did a dumpster dive? You only have to pay me 33% if it works. I will make you look really good in the process. What do you think?"

It is a literal no brainer to them. They aren't even using their list now. To your client, your offer represents all upside and no potential downside. They usually only have one reservation. Typically, they are worried about their reputation. By letting them know you will make them look good, it's an easy and automatic "yes'.

Just like that, you have control of their customers. Of course, for the moment is it *their customer list* and *not yours*.

How do you make that transition? Here's the deeper strategy for being two steps ahead. That's where the unbranded group or unbranded list comes in.

What can we do? Perhaps invite them to a private Facebook group for "Local Deals For Los Angeles Homeowners". Maybe invite them to a VIP email list for special local deals. When they join, guess whose asset it is now? Guess whose list it is?

Let's be really clear here. These people are buyers. Not leads. Not prospects. Not even "highly interested". They have already taken out their credit card and took action. Where are you going to find a more proven list than that?

To top it off, you *start* the list with the relationship they have already cultivated.

What happens when those customers join the unbranded group or list? Whatever you want. You are no longer held prisoner in the box of "I sell roofing".

How hard is it to go to other local businesses and say, "I have a private group of California homeowners. I'd like to offer them a special deal on your products and services. Would you be open to paying me a referral every time you make a sale?"

What do we know about these people? For starters, we know they are homeowners. What else could offer them that helps them? What about other home contracting services? Local food delivery? Insurance? Fireplaces? Gardening and lawn care? Second mortgages? Security systems? Financial planning and investments? Cars? Vacations? Homes for sale in the area? There are no limits, only your imagination.

You can send out as many new offers as you feel like. Plus, by having your own list or group, they will get better deals. You will get them better terms than they could find themselves. It's a great value to them. They love you for selling them more shit.

It still gets better. When you offer those other services, are you the one actually doing the work? Are you swinging a hammer, filing mortgage documents, or dropping off food on their doorstep? Or are you leveraging your knowledge, expertise, and control of strategic assets? Are you getting paid from your strategic thinking?

Travis Sago says, "In short every business is:
1. There is a supply of something (a product asset).
2. You do something to it (a process asset).
3. You sell it to someone (a marketing asset).
4. The persons or distribution channel you sell it to (People assets).

The *closer* you are to the people, the more *valuable* the asset. The *farther* the less valuable the asset. This is why it's a shame people are so product focused. Product is the least valuable and it's best use is to get customers and clients, which are the *most valuable*."

This shift requires you to *think like an investor* instead of as a "service provider". Investors acquire and control under-appreciated and under-valued assets. They maximize their upside and minimize their risk.

Too many people try to automate and streamline a $47 transaction. You want to think differently. If you owned a mortgage note, would you rather get paid $10,000 once or $500/month for 25 years? The wealthiest companies in the world are insurance companies and banks. They always use financing to make their offers affordable. You can offer your assets on payment plans for as long as humanly possible. You can keep getting paid for work you do one time.

Of course, you still get paid along the way for your service. It is not an either or situation. You don't have to sell your service or get control of an asset. You do both at the same time. Just don't lose sight of the real wealth. The real wealth isn't the $1000/month the client is paying you. It is the asset that you are really building for the long term.

That's why the "first date" principle is so powerful. You only commit to winning projects, opportunities, and situations.

Hopefully you are seeing the *true power* of this.

Wealth Shortcut #3 - Bolt Ons/Additions

Do you know the one thing your clients pay more attention to than anything else in the world? Their front end. The 'new'. That's where all the scrutiny and blame goes. If you work on their front end, they will watch you like a hawk.

However, the front end isn't even the most important number. There is probably already flow in their business elsewhere. You can simply harness and multiply that flow. This is what nature does.

For example, which would be easier - get complete strangers to come eat at your client's new restaurant or offer an extra to the people already sitting there?

You probably agree it's easier to do the second option. However, in practice almost everyone does the first option. They go after all the hard money. They go where there is no flow and try to create it. They chase "new".

Nature harnesses and observes flow. Strategic business is the same. Where is the monetary flow now? How can you be an additional value add to what's already there?

Where is the flow already? If this seems like an abstract concept, it isn't. If you're going to take the time to write the 127 page pdf, should you advertise it to strangers on Facebook or offer a bonus inside the members area of another successful course? If you have a small web design firm with 7 paying clients, which should you try - get an 8th paying client or offer something extra to the 7 clients you already have? If you have a course that sold 50 copies, should you create another new course or get more leverage out of the one you've already sold?

Most agencies don't harness the flow. That's because they try to sell "improvement" or "replacement" offers. "Oh that other company is running your Google Adwords? We can *improve* your results." "Oh you don't really like your website? Let's *replace* it with a new one."

Improvement and replacement offers are difficult to sell. They require turning the whole ship around. They are big decisions. Big decisions are easy to say "no" to.

Bolt on or addition offers are easy to sell. They require no turning of the ship. They are tiny decisions. Tiny decisions are easy to say "yes" to.

"Oh you have 7 web design clients? I wonder if they would be interested in adding on a set of matching brochures for their branding? Oh you're selling Google adwords? I wonder if we could add a mystery shopping phone call service to help them close more of the calls they're already getting? Oh you have 50 people booked tonight in your restaurant? I wonder if they would be interested in an additional free dessert coupon for their next visit?"

The only limit is your own imagination. You find the flow and add value. You add on and bolt on to what's already flowing.

If you want to move the needle, think less about replacing and improving. Get away from trying to create a new flow. Instead, think more about adding on to the flow that is already there.

You put your sail into the wind that's already blowing. Unless of course you really love busting your ass off trying to create flow where it's not already. Swimming *with* the current is easier. It's your choice.

Wealth Shortcut #4 - The Leverage To Work Once, Get Paid Again And Again

Years ago our agency was the first one to run Facebook ads for personal injury lawyers. The prevailing wisdom was that people believed only

Google ads could work for them. This was because first they needed someone to be in a car accident. How exactly do you target someone on Facebook who has been in a car accident? You can't.

On Google this was a far easier task. They're searching for them. Why did we not just run Google ads? Because they are crazy expensive for injury lawyers.

On Google, 78 of the 100 most expensive keywords are lawyer keywords. For example, "best mesothelioma attorney" is $1000 per click. If you click it, I think Google sends you a special hat or pin. Plus some bells, a whistle, and balloons. In your average American city, most lawyer keywords are over $200 for a single click.

Facebook leads were far cheaper. Making them work required rolling up our sleeves and really figuring it out. The targeting was trickier.

Eventually we cracked it and we were running profitable ads. Sooner or later, we could repeat those results. It didn't happen overnight.

Why am I sharing this with you? Because guess what happens when we sign a second client? We use the same ads, targeting, landing pages, and everything else. We take what's already working and multiply the results. We multiply the results of a single effort.

Of course, that was in 2016. Knowing what I know now, we would have leveraged it even more. We did not even need to run ads. We could have leased the working intellectual property to lawyers in other cities and states. We could have earned our fees passively through royalty checks instead of service contracts.

We could have also documented the process. We could have a course on how to run Facebook ads for lawyers. We could have taught other agency owners how to do this in other niches. We could have gotten 5 or 6 unique uses out of just one single client result. How many other ways could one success be leveraged into other income streams?

Therein lies the importance of leverage for you. When you do work for a client now, what happens? After your initial effort, does that work continue to pay you again and again? Or do you have to always create new landing pages, campaigns, ads, copy, etc etc?

Right now in your agency you too have underutilized assets. How can you get more use out of what you already have? How can you take what's already working and reuse, recycle, reinvent, and reimagine?

How much more could you get done if one client paid for you 50? You don't have to change what you're doing. You can still trade client services for money. You just want to think about getting more use out of what you've already created.

Do you design a client's web page? What if you standardized it as a theme and resold the rights on a popular wordpress themes website? What if you leased the creatives to other designers in non-competing niches?

Have you figured out how to get $8 Facebook leads with a single pdf? What if you lease it to non-competitors in other geographic areas? Did you get some webinar registrations for your coaching client? What if you documented it and made a mini course for other coaches to model?

Most agencies do all work custom and build everything from scratch. Most of your clients don't need custom work. They just think they do.

Think about getting more uses out of what you're already doing. You already put in the effort. You might as well get paid for it again and again.

The 4 Wealth Shortcuts Multiply Your Results

These 4 principles take you out of the big trap most agency owners and freelancers fall into. They trade time for money in the form of their services. They are building themselves a high-paying job, of which there is no escape. This takes away your freedom to be with the people that matter most.

These 4 principles delink the imprisonment structure. It's a structure that says every client must mean more work. The principles also change your focus. Instead of working at the hardest and most difficult part of the business, you do it differently. You don't create flow. You harness it. You multiply what already works.

Because when you get strategic, you pick up assets out of the trash, you control and improve assets, you create strategic additions and bolt on offers, and you leverage your results to get paid repeatedly on one effort. That's when your accelerated wealth is inevitable.

Even better if you reinvest your money after you earn it. My favorite short term asset is underpriced land. My favorite long term asset is a global share of the stock market in the Vanguard 500 fund.

These principles really are a 30 year wealth shortcut. Your average hedge fund owner is 30 years old. They take on clients who are generally over 65 years old. Often that older person has taken 30 years to accumulate that kind of wealth. The hedge fund manager controls the asset and gets paid on it rain or shine. The hedge fund manager controls it with leverage because he does the same thing for everybody's money. Think more like a hedge fund manager and less like a web designer.

This is a path for you to get true wealth. The kind of wealth where you actually have the time and freedom to enjoy it.

Chapter 11: The Journey Of Purpose, Ayahuasca, And A Perfect Average Day

In 2010, I had my first ayahuasca experience. If you're not familiar with ayahuasca, western medicine calls it "the world's most powerful hallucinogenic drug". For over 5000 years, natives in the Amazon jungle have used it as part of their shamanism healing rituals.

They say that drinking ayahuasca gives one direct access to the spirit world. Ayahuasca translates to "vine of the soul" or the "vine of the dead".

It contains a chemical called DMT, which is what your body makes during REM sleep and during a near death experience. In truth, it is not just a drug or just a spirit journey. It is both.

When I first heard about this fascinating compound, researching it became an obsession of mine. In 2010 ayahuasca was far less "mainstream". You had to really dig for information.

Miracles Of Spirit

I kept reading stories that were utterly mind-blowing. Often people would have miraculous healings accompanied by intense life-altering experiences. One person had a lifelong depression cured in a single experience. They told wild stories of puking out demons and seeing visions of God. Another person had their vision restored after a life of blindness. Another person had their cancer instantaneously healed.

It wasn't just that they had cured the incurable. The people always came back talking about spirits, afterlife, angelic beings, pure peace and love, and a deeper sense of reality. The more I read the more I wanted to know.

I was in an interesting predicament in my life. Growing up both my parents were alcoholics. My mom was an unsupported single mother who got burnt out. I saw my dad once every 6 months. Being there wasn't really his thing. I was very "anti-drugs" because I didn't want to go down that same road.

My mother stuck to just the booze. On the other hand, my dad had tried every drug under the sun.

My childhood was mostly a collection of traumas and drugs were a central player. There was always a questionable cast of characters moving through my story.

I saw far too many things that a 10 year old shouldn't see. You shouldn't know what heroine is at 9 years old. Many times I had my stuff stolen. This led to a very opinionated me that said "all drugs are bad".

Yet somehow ayahuasca seemed different. I couldn't explain. I just knew I had to try it once in my life. I didn't know how or when. I just knew that I was meant to try it.

I Finally Took The Plunge

In 2010 I discovered you can legally buy ayahuasca online. They ship it right to your doorstep. There are two components in an ayahuasca tea. Neither component does anything without the other one. It is only illegal to combine them.

The first component is a DMT-containing leaf commonly called Chacruna. The other is the ayahuasca vine itself, which contains no active drugs.

Our stomachs contain an enzyme that normally breaks down DMT before any effect is experienced. However, the ayahuasca vine has a chemical called an MAO-inhibitor, which prevents the stomach from breaking down the DMT. You need the MAO-inhibitor and the DMT together. Once combined they make for one hell of a journey.

In my first experience, I followed what the internet recommended verbatim. Knowing what I know, I would not buy it online. I would only recommend you use it with an experienced shaman. At the time, I wasn't wise enough to know what I was getting myself into it.

In my first experience, I tried a very tiny "introductory dose". I experienced a few pretty colors but nothing significant.

The second time I took a little bit more. More pretty colors but it was also nothing life-changing.

The Experience That Changed Everything

The third time was the beginning of something incredible which continues to this day. It was my first ever "hallucinatory" experience. I remember the walls around me started to flow and become alive like the waves of the ocean. It was immensely colorful and pretty but the beginning wasn't anything profound.

I felt disappointed yet again. Online I had read all these incredible ayahuasca stories. Yet here I was just seeing a few pretty colors. I remember thinking in my head, "Where is my miraculous healing?" Then boom it hit me like a ton of bricks!

It was one of the weirdest experiences I have ever had, if not the weirdest. It's as if it physically took over my body. I was sitting on my couch, staring forward into space. When suddenly my right arm lunged down, yanked a kleenex box off the ground, and ferociously pulled it an inch from my face. Whoa! Freaked out I said, "Whatever that was, don't do that again." I pushed the kleenex box away with my other free hand.

I began again, "Where is my miraculous healing?" Again suddenly my right arm lunged down to the ground and yanked the kleenex box towards my face. It was entirely bizarre. I used my left hand to push it away again.

This happened 5 times in a row. Finally said, "Okay I'll look at it." I gazed into the kleenex box. Suddenly something unexpected happened.

The kleenex box had outer space patterns overlaid with the words, "Of dreams and inspirations". Suddenly out of nowhere, the words began to shimmer. In a few seconds they became 3-dimensional. Then they floated right off the kleenex box. In my vision, I watched as the words slowly floated right into the center of my being. The minute those words "hit me", I felt instantly inspired. It wasn't just the word "inspiration", I had embodied its meaning. I felt so beautifully free.

The Universe Inside The Kleenex Box

I stared deeper into the kleenex box. The outer space pattern inside began to look three dimensional. It was like I was looking into a little tiny universe inside of my kleenex box. I felt like Galileo or Copernicus must have felt as they discovered the cosmos for the first time.

I lost myself for hours just watching this kleenex universe expand and create. Galaxies flowed, worlds collided, and new stars were colorfully born. I lost myself deeper into the tiny kleenex world. If a cop was around, I surely would have been arrested. There was just some weirdo tripping balls staring into a kleenex box. You don't exactly see that every day. Thankfully I was safe at home on my own couch.

With my online supply, I drank ayahuasca 6 times over two years by myself. Then the story took a wildly interesting turn.

The next day I was again stone cold sober. Yet this visionary experience somehow continued. I started repeatedly seeing the same synchronicity again and again; a blue butterfly.

11:11, Blue Butterflies, And Synchronicities

Every single day, I would see different blue butterflies 15-20 per day. This continued every day for over 2 years. If you've ever walked by the clocks and it was 11:11 or 1:11, you have probably had a similar experience. Except this same sign was happening to me repeatedly. It happened in so many unusual ways. I would not have believed it myself had I not actually experienced it.

Someone mentioned a prominent psychedelic author and speaker named Terence McKenna. They suggested I check him out. I opened a Youtube video and his t-shirt was a blue butterfly.

Another time at the grocery story, my girlfriend asked me to grab a vegetable tray. I managed to pick up a veggie tray off the shelf without noticing it. When I got home, the tray itself was a blue butterfly. There were different cut up vegetables in each part of the wing.

Another time I was checking out books on Amazon. Something interesting caught my eye. It was a book about near death experiences. Of course, more blue butterflies. There was a butterfly on the front cover.

There was seemingly nowhere I could hide. I remember watching a porn video. The girl bent over and on her ass was a big fat blue butterfly tramp stamp.

When A Video Game Becomes Reality

Then there was my most memorable synchronicity. My girlfriend bought me a Nintendo Wii game called Skyward Sword. It is part of the Legend of Zelda series, which was always my favorite game as a kid. Playing Zelda is a full excuse for me to geek out and disconnect from reality for a week.

The game started out as a pretty typical "save the princess" kind of game. You're the typical sword-wielding good guy, presumably trying to get laid by the hot princess. Of course, as it went on the game only got weirder and more synchronistic from there.

Within the game there were these beautiful meadows. In the meadows, there would be 3 or 4 blue butterflies. The butterflies floated around each other, weaving a little circle. I remember thinking, "Here we go with more blue butterflies."

About 3-4 hours into the game, it takes a wild detour. Your character gets knocked unconscious and while you are out cold, the princess goes missing.

You wake up hours later with a spirit over your bed. The spirit says, "I can't explain why but you just come with me right now. I have something important to show you."

The spirit then takes you down a secret pathway to a hidden temple. Inside the temple she teaches you a sacred medicine song. She says, "This is a sacred healing song passed down from spirits. You must play your song where the blue butterflies gather."

Deeper Down The Rabbit Hole

This story gets more synchronistic still. You find the circling blue butterflies and sing your medicine song. At that point, one of three possible things happens. Either a stone pops out of the ground and imparts upon you some deep ancient wisdom. Secondly, hearts shoot out and your character collects them to have his full health restored. Finally, a gateway opens and you leave your physical body to go on a journey of spirit. On these spirit journeys, you acquire items and knowledge that can be used within the real game.

These non-physical journeys were powerful. For me, that Zelda game story became quite literal. Because that's what actually happened to me. More on that in a second.

The sixth time I tried ayahuasca on my own was intense. I decided I was ready to go deep. I was ready for a real spiritual experience. I was no longer content with a few pretty colors. I wanted answers.

Drinking Enough Ayahuasca To Kill A Small Elephant

I brewed my ayahuasca tea 50-100 times as strong as the internet recommended. There was no turning back.

I still remember my little prayer of intention before I drank. It was quite simple and to the point. "Please God don't fucking kill me."

It took me over an hour to summon the courage to drink it. Partly because ayahuasca is the most foul tasting brew you have ever consumed. Partly because I was utterly scared shitless.

Then the visions began. At some point, I had a vision of a massive blue butterfly. It was made up of millions of tiny blue butterflies.

By this point, the sheer number of blue butterflies in my reality was getting eerie. What did it mean? If the universe was trying to tell me something, I wasn't getting the message.

Hours later I was finally sobering up. I had enough wherewithal to make sense of all these blue butterflies. I decided to do what any savvy internet nerd would do. I googled that shit. What else was I going to do, right?

Only one search result came up. There was an ayahuasca retreat in Peru that used the Blue

Butterfly at their logo. I knew instantly I was meant to go there.

Months later I went down to the Amazon jungle to drink ayahuasca. It was my first time with a master shaman. In December of 2012, I had my first real undeniable mystical experience.

The retreat center I went to is known for having the strongest ayahuasca anywhere. They also have a 'home brew' they used privately for training shamans. The home brew is anywhere from 2-4 times as strong as the normal brew. The normal brew is already legendary strong ayahuasca. The maximum dosage they ever give anyone is a full cup. I drank a full cup of the home brew.

I thought I knew what strong ayahuasca was. I had no fucking idea.

In many ways, you could say I tried the strongest dose of the world's strongest drug by the world's strongest provider. It made for a pretty eventful night.

The First Mystical Experience

Intense does not even begin to describe my experience. In a typical ayahuasca experience, you drink and about an hour later you experience the effects. There is a time delay before you feel anything. On a full cup of the home brew, I was tripping balls seconds later. It hit me harder than anything I had ever experienced before.

The experience went on for an eternity. It grew and grew and grew in intensity. At least 100 times I was sure I was dying. I eventually reached a place where everything was one eternal unending infinite loving creation.

The experience was beyond any words I had to describe it. There was no time, no separation, no end, and no beginning. Everything was utter loving perfection. In all the cosmos, not even a single grain of sand was out of place. I radiated an infinite loving peace to all beings everywhere.

I had questions answered I had wondered my whole life. I saw why everything was, down to why my curtains were red in my first childhood house. Everything was magically connected in an eternal dance without end or beginning.

"Hallucination" is not the right word to describe it. Reality did not "stop". It grew. This reality just became a subset of something bigger and more profound. An infinite game of life that never ends.

I experienced a deeper part of reality in a way I will never forget. That night I released a lifelong depression and anxiety. I can remember the exact moment in time when I let go my last ever panic attack.

I experienced colors I had never experienced before, sounds that created worlds, colorful beings that radiated pure love, and just a deep knowing that it was all okay always.

Since then, I have had over 500 of these types of mystical experiences. Many were on substances and many of them were experienced while stone cold sober. It was like once I found that 'place' within the plants, I could remember how to access it. I didn't need anything to "go back". Pretty crazy story, right?

What Does This Have To Do With Business?

What does any of that have to do with running a digital marketing agency? Absolutely everything.

Before that night, I was at a point in my agency mostly running SEO campaigns for plastic surgeons. I also ran some Google Adwords campaigns.

At some point, I had an eternity to look at my life and what I really wanted. I realized that running campaigns wasn't what I really wanted to do with my life. I didn't want my tombstone to say, "He was good at building backlinks."

In ayahuasca, you often purge physically by vomiting. I literally vomited up my SEO agency. I decided to let it go to pursue something more meaningful. I was afraid to lose it. I didn't know what I would do instead. However, I realized something. The skills I had learned would continue to serve me forever. If anything, the business was just evolving into a better place.

When you have an eternity to be real with yourself, a few funny things happen. You get to ask yourself a lot of deep meaningful questions. Why am I doing this? Is this how I really imagined my life? Is this what I really want? What would truly make me happy? When my life comes to an end, what kind of difference do I want to have made in this world?

Do You Love It Or Is It Just A Means To An End?

I realized that I really did love something about agency work. I loved getting paid steady regular income every month. I loved the feeling I got from really helping someone. I loved contributing to a business that truly added something to this planet. I loved the freedom of being able to work from a laptop anywhere in the world with internet. I loved some of my clients very dearly.

I also realized that a lot of it just wasn't working for me. It was really just a means to make money. In fact, lots of the things were the bane of my existence.

I hated having client phone calls that were often like an interrogation. I hated feeling like I had bosses. I hated building backlinks and staring at a computer screen all day. I hated being dependent on Google. I hated that every new client meant I had more grunt work. I hated that some clients would leave disappointed and I would carry that on my conscience.

I hated that it was a thankless job and nobody ever really appreciated the hard work I put in for them. Most of all, I hated that I had no control over my own life. If a client wanted to talk on a Sunday night, I never truly felt like I could say no. I hated that I wasn't really free.

Designing Your Agency To Serve Your Life

What about your own agency? Even if these types of experiences aren't for you, you can still benefit from them. Because one thing is for sure. You most definitely can have a digital marketing agency *your way*.

You can have the parts you actually like without all the parts that suck. Most people just accept those parts. You don't have to.

Here are a few ideas you can take from these experiences.

What Is Your Life Purpose?

Why do you wake up each day and do what you do? Is this how you truly want to make your mark on this planet? Personally, my highest value is freedom. I believe a life with freedom is the only life worth lived. The bigger purpose of this book is to give you back your freedom.

What do you stand for? What makes you feel truly passionate and alive?

Finding your purpose doesn't work like most people think it does. Most people think you "discover" your purpose. That is a serious misconception and people get stuck looking for what cannot be found.

Purpose, like all things, is created. It is a choice. You can choose to create purpose for yourself or you can live without one.

The Single Most Important Choice You Make

Before you can decide what is your purpose, you must decide *who* is your purpose. Who do you really want to work with? Who are the clients who really inspire you? Who makes you want to get up out of bed and do something to better this world?

Because who you work with makes all the difference in the world. The right people appreciate you, you get them results, they are fun to be around, you laugh with them, you can just be yourself, and you know you're making a difference.

If you choose the wrong people, you will spend a lot of your time feeling guilty, feeling obligated to them, feeling their disappointment, being fake, and dreading every interaction with them.

You cannot live purposely without purposely impacting other people. Who you choose to work with matters more than any other decision you make.

Who Is Your Perfect Who?

Your perfect client is not merely an academic exercise. Think back for a moment. Who is a client you truly loved serving? What made them a wonderful client? How cool would it be to only have to help people just like them? What were their values that you shared?

I bet they were easy to help, fun to interact with, said thanks, and paid you a lot. What else made them a great client for you?

Now think back about your worst clients. Who is a client you just didn't vibe with? What made them a crappy client for you? Were there warning signs there that you didn't see at the time?

I bet they were rude, demanding, didn't see your value, had unrealistic expectations, blamed you, and were unwilling to help themselves. What else made them a bad client?

Now look at all the things that made your bad client a bad client. Then look at all the things that made your great clients great. Notice any patterns?

Decide on your who. Because when you get clear on this central issue, you intentionally choose the clients that make sense for you.

Grab a pen and paper for this next part.

The Perfect Client Exercise

What makes your perfect client a perfect client? It is a combination of two things.

1. Their attitude (80%)
2. Their situation (20%)

On a blank sheet of paper, draw a line down the middle. On the left side, we are going to write the traits of your best clients. On the right side, we are going to look at the traits of your worst clients.

Your past leaves clues. The goal of this exercise is not to live in fantasy land. Think about actual clients you have had. You want to talk about real people with real names. You want to evaluate real situations you have worked in.

What made the good ones good? What made the bad ones bad? Stop reading for a moment to write down your answers.

Attitude Is A Choice

Start with their attitudes first. What made the good clients good? What made the bad ones bad? What were their attitudes when you worked together? Write down your answers so you can see the differences. Pause for a moment to reflect as you write these down.

What Problem Did You Solve?

Next we want to look at your client's situations. What was happening in their situation when they contacted you? Why did they call you?

Look at someone you really helped in the past. What problem did you solve? What did you do for them that really helped them? Pause for a moment and write down your answers.

What if the attitudes and the situations you enjoyed were different people in different situations? It's totally okay. We want to get a clear picture of the attitudes and situations in which you can weave your magic. We want to see what problems you enjoy solving and for who you love solving them.

The more you do this exercise, the clearer you will get. You want to know the right person and the right situation for you. You should be equally clear about who you should *not* be working with.

One of the best financial decisions you can make is to say "no". Be willing to say "no" to any client who is on the wrong side of your paper. This can be hard when someone has a credit card in hand ready to pay you. Be uncompromising in your high standards. Because it is not the money alone you are saying "no" to. You are saying "no" to a bad situation, a bad attitude, or a problem you do not enjoy solving. Rejecting the wrong clients will make your job later infinitely easier.

Hell Yes Or Hell No?

If you are not an enthusiastic 100% "hell yes" about any client, opportunity, or situation, then you are a "no". Don't settle for less. It's either "hell yes" or it's a "no". There is no in between. You deserve a "hell yes" lifestyle.

The 5 Critical Questions Of Your Purpose

Now that you are clearer about the right who, let's go a few levels deeper. Let's dive into your true purpose.

There are 5 specific clarity questions you must have clear answers to. By having that clarity, you will love what you do for a living. Because specific clarity gives you the power to do what you are truly meant to do. It will put you inside of your zone of genius. This is where you make maximum impact with minimum effort. This is where your results flow with effortless ease.

Always remember, you are not meant to do everything. You are meant to double down on your strengths. Where you are weak, others are naturally strong. What you do not enjoy, others love. Everything that is not 100% "hell yes" should be outsourced.

1. Who do I most love to work with and help?
2. What do I really love to do?
3. What am I really good at?
4. What does the world really need?
5. How can I get paid to do that?

The center of your answers is a magic place where these questions overlap for you.

Don't be theoretical with your answers. Your past experience leaves clues. Who should you work with in the future? Who do you already love working with now? What will you love doing? What do you already love doing now? Pause and write down your answers.

If you want to know who you should help tomorrow, look at who you already love helping today. If you want to know what you're good at, look at what problems you already solve now.

What Does The World Need From You?

The fourth question, understanding your market's needs, is a bit unique. You cannot answer that all by yourself. You must spend some time actually *listening* to your market.

The best resource is to ask your actual clients about problems they have. You can also read Facebook groups or Amazon reviews. You want to find conversations that get a lot of traction and get upvoted a lot. That is your market saying to you, "Here's what you should be paying attention to."

Get clear on the answers to these questions for yourself. Know your why. Know yourself.

What Is Your Perfect Average Day?

Most entrepreneurs have goals. In general, goals are a good practice. I run a private goal writing group on Facebook. The problem is the way most people create goals leads to them being disappointed.

Not all your goals will have an equal impact. There is a special kind of goal that you need to work towards: process goals.

Most people set external results goals. They want to make more money. They want to sign more clients. They want the house and the Porsche. For the record, I'm not saying you shouldn't have those goals. You should. It's just that process goals trump them all.

How Process Goals Work

Imagine two people. One named Tall Tree Teddy and another named Watering Walter.

Teddy has a goal to create a 10 foot tall tree. He puts pictures of the tree on his vision board and busts his ass towards it daily. He writes his goal about a 10 foot tall tree every day.

Walter has a process goal to water trees. Somewhere in his journey, he discovered that he really just loves watering trees. Gardening for him is a true blessing. He finds it a lot like meditation.

Every day he waters a tree, he is doing what he loves. Walter has no goals whatsoever to create a big tree. He waters trees just for the love of gardening.

In 3 years time, who do you think will have a 10 foot tall tree? Who will have inevitably hit the goal? I've witnessed many Teddy's give up while Walter just keeps plugging away. The Walters almost always end up with 10 foot tall trees. Plus they just keep going. Switch out a $1,000,000 agency for a tree and the story is every bit as factual.

How do you most love spending a day? How can you design your perfect average day? How can you design a life that is spent on your terms? What processes are their own reward for you? What processes automatically create the outcomes that you want?

It is extremely important that you focus on an "average" day. Sure you may have a day where you skydive from 15,000 feet, land in the Playboy mansion, snort cocaine off a dozen models' asses, and drive a Ferrari at mach speed to your yacht. But that's not sustainable. Most of your days aren't going to be like that.

Design your average day on purpose. Then you design your agency to fit into your life around your perfect average day. Your agency should support your time and life. It should not own your time. It should not own you.

A Cool Ass Totally Normal Day

To give you a sense of what's possible, here's what this looks like in my family. In the last 3 years, we have visited over 30 countries. Some we visited for months and others just a few days. We did whatever we felt like.

I've made two beautiful baby girls. My daughters are Heidi and Zelda.

Each morning begins with a prayer of thanks for what we have. I give my baby girls a hug and a smile. I let them know that they are loved. My lady gets an extra sexy kiss, sometimes with morning breath, somethings without.

We all lay in bed together and have cuddle time for an hour. Firstly, I read a few great books that have been recommended by other great entrepreneurial friends. I like reading a chapter or two out of several different books. Then I read some Dr Seuss to my daughters and anything else they ask me to. We always get new books for family reading time.

We make a fresh homemade green vegetable juice. I spend about 30 minutes visualizing and connecting with what I want to accomplish. Then we all make a nice healthy breakfast together.

Around 11 am, I work for 2 hours on what's most important. I focus on the processes that I enjoy which directly create outcomes I also desire. Usually I work when both my girls are off for a nap. I send a few messages to our team to catch up on where we're at.

Then I will spend 10 minutes reading up on the issues of my marketplace. I reach out to a few friends and close colleagues. We go for an afternoon family walk together in nature. I bring a pen and a paper to organize my best ideas. As a rule, we don't bring any phones or technology. We like to be present with each other.

Sometimes my lady and I have sex in the middle of the day. It's a special treat. I'm sure our neighbors love us for it.

Later in the afternoon I work on learning something new. Lately I've been learning piano and German, French, and Spanish. I also read up on investing, which is something I am getting into more and more.

At night, we all have a healthy delicious dinner together. We usually take a family bath together in our hot tub.

I will play some songs on my guitar for my girls while they dance. We share lots of laughs and enjoy our time together.

Because this is an average day, it is perfectly sustainable. Each of those items takes just a few minutes to enjoy. I genuinely feel blessed because I am. Although I am extremely fortunate, I am not "lucky". I have directly chosen these experiences. You can choose your experience in the same way.

What Processes Bring You Joy?

What does your perfect day look like? What are the parts of the business that light you up? What do you truly love doing? How can you make your business work for your life?

How can you accomplish more by doing less? How can you contribute something big and meaningful to your clients? What kind of habits and routines would you need to support that? What processes make your outcomes inevitable? How can you systematize and organize those habits so they are easy and efficient? Who can help you achieve that faster, easier, and better?

What is the perfect average day *for you*?

Chapter 12: Building A Team of A+ Superstars Who Make You Look Like A God

Would you love to be able to delegate more tasks? Do you ever struggle handing off because of quality? Do clients ever want you specifically for the quality you bring?

Do you feel like delegating means you would need to hire a rockstar? Do you think that a rockstar would be too costly? Have you had a lot of negative experiences before with freelancers in third world countries?

Hiring Success Secrets

If you're at the stage of hiring freelancers and staff, you already know your decision can make or break your progress. *Who* you hire is by far your biggest success factor.

If you hire the wrong person, they will make your life miserable and stressful. You won't be able to trust them to do a good job. You'll always have to micromanage them. The quality will suffer.

When you have to micromanage people, every decision in your business will depend on you. Your limited time and attention will slow you down. You will become your own company's bottleneck.

If it feels easier just to do everything yourself, alarm bells should be going off in your head. It means you don't have an A+ fit. You can't grow if you have to carry every single task on your shoulders. Carrying your entire business means you also will get burnt out sooner than later. In the long term, your sanity depends on having good people you can trust to do a great job the first time.

Most people get stuck with B and C level players. B and C players usually have a "just enough" attitude. They are just looking for any job. They do the bare minimum. They often aren't so bad that you would want to fire them. You will also never be blown away by their performance. They will doom your agency to mediocrity. Don't settle for 'just okay' people.

On the other hand, a superstar will take a big weight off your shoulders. You can trust them to do it right the first time. In fact, a superstar will do it better than you could have done it yourself. They may not be able to run the whole business as well as you do. However, when it comes to their one piece, they are excellent at it.

Employees Should Be "Hell Yes" Or No

Don't settle for anything less than a great fit. The right people have a 'can do' positive attitude. They believe in your bigger mission. They want their results to speak for themselves. With the right people you can relax and let go when it's in their hands. You almost don't need to manage them at all.

The hardest part is not finding them, it's in you letting go. It is not putting everything on yourself. It is thinking about what you do as a real business and not as a freelancer providing service.

Of course, hiring is a tricky slope. No one has all the answers. You will make some mistakes along the way. We all do.

I once had to fire a bad employee for watching cartoon porn on the job. Twice. Yep. The first time was pretty shocking. The second time he knew he was being watched. He even had to click a button on his time tracking software to login to work, which then recorded his screen. Maybe he liked being watched. Who knows?

Nothing says you can't work here anymore quite like, "Hey so I checked your work output today and saw a cartoon Japanese chick getting fucked by an octopus. Call me crazy but I don't think that was research for your article."

My first employee was a freelance writer. He was a really nice guy and a terrible employee. For every 10 minutes of writing he did, I had to do another 20 minutes of editing. I hired him because he was a cheap virtual assistant. Because I couldn't pay much, I felt like I had to settle for broken english articles. In the end, I realized he was making my life harder rather than easier. The right employees should always lighten your workload, not add to it.

I have also had great employees who understood exactly what I wanted. Great people get things done right the first time. They produce work that turns out amazingly well. They are self-responsible. You don't need to look over their shoulder to make sure they are doing a good job. The clients always love their positive upbeat demeanor. I have also had those amazing people. You can't lose with people like that.

Here are 5 shortcuts so you get an A+ fit on your team the first time.

1. Have A Clear Defined Mission.

A+ players are usually buying into your *why* more than your *what*. It's not what your company does but why they do it. They aren't there just to show up and collect a paycheck. They want to know their work is valued. They want to make a difference. They want to do something exciting. They want a valued use of their natural gifts and abilities.

If you can't articulate your company mission beyond "we exist to make money", you won't retain A players. Your mission should be written out, clear and concise. If you called any employee in the middle of the night, their stumbling, fumbling mouth should be able to recite your company mission.

Your mission gets everybody working towards the same goal. If your goal is to be "number one in client service", would it make sense to hire an arm-twisting smooth-talking inauthentic salesperson? Or would you be better served investing into your department of gratitude so you can generate more referrals? These decisions get easier when you have a clear picture of the mission. It also makes it easier to get your freelancers and employees to take on your values.

If you mostly work alone and only hire the occasional freelancer, a mission statement may not seem all that important. In actuality, you can't sustain growth without it. If you want to earn more and impact more, you need one.

A clear, concise 2-3 sentence mission will also get you clear on the type of people you need. What is your mission?

2. Pay 5-10% Above Market.

Top talents have choice. You can't cheapskate your way into great people. Having said that, you don't have to break the bank either. If an average virtual assistant makes $350/month, be willing to pay $380-400/month.

The right people aren't trying to get rich off of you. They want to feel well compensated and better off than they would be elsewhere.

Depending on the position, it may make sense to pay them entirely on performance. Be willing to pay a little bit more to tilt the talent pool in your direction. Find out what market value is and be willing to go a little above it.

3. Screen For The Right People In Your Job Posting.

What is a job posting *really*? It is an ad that sells why your company would be a cool place to work. It is not actually a "job posting" at all. It is your digital brochure that says, "Here's the cool mission that we're building."

Your job ads should scream, "If you're an up and coming superstar with our shared values, come join us." As much as possible, you want to be extremely real about what kind of person you need. Speaking in generalities won't bring the right people.

If you want someone to answer the phone 7x per hour say so. If you want to grow and aren't sure what their role will be in 6 months say so. Just be real with people. People respect honesty.

You want to avoid generic traditional résumé babble. That only works to attract mediocre talent. Don't say generic crap like "works well in a team as well as on solo projects." It's too unspecific to stand any chance of getting the right person. Those types of ads unconsciously say "come on in B and C level players".

Think about how most people recruit. Most people end up with B and C players. Don't model losers. Model winners. Model great companies hiring processes.

One of my wisest mentors always liked making people do something different in his job ad. Sometimes he would have you write a unique phrase on your cover letter. There's nothing quite like writing, "Hello my name is Frankie and I really love eating apples". Strange as it sounds, it shows you actually read the ad and you know how to follow instructions.

Remember that most potential employees are just looking for any old job to put in half an effort. They don't care who pays them or what they do. As long as they can make a rent payment and get drunk on Friday, they will accept any job. You want to push those people away intentionally.

Adding this little extra screening step helps avoid the wrong people. You will avoid people who don't care about you or your company. You will avoid that churn and burn employee mentality.

You can even have people do a sample mini task. What better way to test them than to have them do a real 5-15 minute example task? Might as well give them a taste of what's to come later, right?

I once had no time and needed a meaningful gift for a client. In my job posting, I had people submit what they would buy for under $50 for a new client. I found the gift I needed. I also found the right person. We were on the same page even before we started. Even before the interview, I got a feel for how we might work together.

4. Don't Interview. Audition.

If you were looking for someone to be in your band, which would you do - ask for a résumé about their last 5 bands or just play together and see what happens? They could talk for hours about their last band and what computer skills they have. You would still learn more with 5 minutes of playing together.

Most people's hiring process doesn't actually make sense. Don't copy everyone else's job interview format just because that's how they do it. Instead of asking your potential candidates some otherwise meaningless questions, create some art together. Have an audition. A simple $5-$100 trial assignment will tell you infinitely more than any interview question.

Think less about "what should I ask them". Think more about "what can we do together in 20-30 minutes to see if we might be a good fit together." Just like a good band. Audition your talent.

5. First Date Each Other Before Marriage.

Most companies hand over a job, give lackluster training, and then they hope they will magically end up with someone great. It almost never works like that. Even if they stumble onto a superstar, they will probably dull his spirit and bore him to death. Again, don't model most average companies. Model the great ones.

Never just hand anyone a job. Offer a chance to work together on a first date basis. Over the long term, the total arrangement has to work for you and everyone involved.

Depending on what you're hiring for, the ideal length of a first date can vary. It can be anywhere from 1 small project to 60 days together.

Feeling each other out first is a winning formula. You want to see you work well together in the trenches. You can also give many first dates for the same job. I have given as many as 20 people trial assignments for one job. Then I have given a second date to the top 4 or 5. You will see the obvious performance differences, which helps you choose someone great.

The reality is most employees just want any old job. You never want people who will do the bare minimum to not get fired. You want someone who loves being part of your team.

"First dates" also create a powerful psychological framework. It's kind of like being a starting quarterback in the NFL. What happens if the starting QB doesn't go out there and prove himself every day? He knows the backup will come in and take his job. That's why he goes out to earn his breaks and prove himself day after day. He puts it all on the line day after day. He never just takes what he has for granted.

You want your staff to have that same hunger to prove themselves. They shouldn't feel like any comfy cozy job has been given. They should still feel like they have to go out and deliver.

Of course, see your teammates as assets to grow with. Be willing to invest in them and train them. There are a few exceptions. If you are hiring for a speciality skill set like Facebook ads or programming, they should already have that training. Otherwise, it is your job to build your team's skills up. Inspire them. Motivate them. Bring out the best in them. Always bring it back to your mission and your vision.

Be an employer who brings out their positive side. As often as you can, let them know they have done a good job. You want to create a wow experience for clients. You can't do that unless you also create a wow experience for your employees. You would be amazed at what a $25 Starbucks gift card and sincere "thank you" will do for team morale and performance.

Maximizing Upside And Minimizing Downside

These are the 5 best principles for hiring and retaining superstars. You want great people who do a great job the first time. Everyone makes a hiring mistake from time to time. With a first date process, you will minimize the damage to just a bad first date. You don't have to commit to months of unnecessary bad hires. You will end up with really good people with relatively minimal effort. Those superstars will rock you and your clients experiences and results.

Managing Your People Proactively On Purpose

If you're in the managing stage, you are no longer doing any of the daily work. Your day is largely spent managing your team and getting the most out of them.

Most of the time you're going to get the same question all day long. It sounds something like this.

"Hey, do you got a minute?"

As a manager, you quickly become the bottleneck in the business. This is because every decision depends on you. You can't scale and grow so long as everything waits for an answer from you.

It is necessary at this stage to remove you from the equation. You have to make less decisions but more important ones.

When it comes to managing, most people are solving the wrong problems. The wrong problems are the ones employees bring to you in the moment. They are almost never high priority issues. That is managing *reactively*.

You want to manage *proactively*. In your business, the right problems are the ones that your data tells you are the critically important leverage points.

Which decisions are the critical and important ones? Only data can tell you that. You must know your numbers. This tells you the right problems to work on. In every agency, about 5-10 key performance indicators tell you what you should be focused on.

What Defines Your Performance?

What are the 5-10 key performance indicators that define your agency? You want to spell those out so everyone knows what's important. Get your team working on the right issues, not just the seemingly most pressing ones. Rarely is what's urgent truly important. Otherwise you can spend all day working on issues and actually accomplishing nothing.

Let's say you want to be the number one agency in client service. If you're having problems keeping clients longer than 6 months, that's a big issue. A logo question from your designer might not be nearly as important as your company response time to phone calls and emails. If you're going to call a team meeting, what's better to work on - the logo or the retention issue? Leaders get everyone on the team working on the right issue together.

Be aware that the data alone won't solve your problems for you. It is like a magnifying glass. It will tell you what problems are worth your time and attention to solve. It will show your team what's important to your company.

The right people working on the right problem can solve any issue.

Chapter 13: Uncertainty, Coronavirus, & Depressed Economies

This special chapter is dedicated to winning in otherwise difficult uncertain financial times. When you can prosper in the hard times, you are financially indestructible.

My agency began in 2007 during an intense recession. My hometown of Windsor, Ontario, Canada lives and dies by the automotive industry. In 2008, I can remember multiple layoff announcements of 10,000+ workers. In a small town, 15% of people losing their jobs is an economic nuclear bomb. The layoffs created a ripple effect that crushed the overall job market.

I was sleeping on my girlfriend's couch, mostly feeling like a total loser. Her father was insistent that I "go get a real job". The thing was nobody was hiring. I went to several headhunters and hiring agencies, who promptly kicked me out the door because they had nothing to offer. Then I went to a few job fairs, and found just commission-only sales jobs.

It Was A Big Life Crossroad

Truthfully, I needed money to survive in a big way. After 8 months, a friend in education told me they had an opening as a janitor. It was $22/hour plus health benefits.

Desperate for any kind of income, I felt like I couldn't say no. In the end, I turned it down. Despite all the judgment I faced, I knew I was put on this earth for more. I knew my days weren't meant to be cleaning up a clogged corn-filled shitty toilet in the boy's locker room. Call me crazy.

Admittedly, it was a ballsy decision to make. On one hand, there was the secure easy road of a steady paycheck. On the other hand, my back was against the wall. It meant I had to make my agency work. There was no more plan B or safety net. Obviously, since you're reading this book, the story has a happy ending. It wasn't always easy though. At times, this path will make you question your sanity.

In difficult economic times, it's usually the freelancers and marketing agencies who are the first ones to go. If you can win in the hardest of times, you will be smooth sailing in the good times.

From 6 Figures Months To Zero

As I write this book, I just spoke to Kate and her entire business was eliminated by coronavirus in a matter of weeks. She has only had a few strategy sessions. No enrollments. It was a pretty steep fall from consistent $100,000 months to zero overnight.

She helps overworked corporate women to stop grinding out 80 hour weeks. The problem is there are almost no corporate women working 80 hour weeks anymore.

The problem she was solving was no longer a need in the market today. She tried out a new Facebook ads agency. I expect the same dismal results. Because she has a deeper problem than just Facebook ads.

Of course, I'm not in Kate's business. However, there are a few things she can do to right her ship. She can find out what her existing customers need now and sell that. She can adjust to what the remaining corporate women need. Most importantly, she can create a recurring offer so she doesn't start every month at zero.

The Missing Piece

Dan Kennedy says, "It's only during hard times that you see who is truly naked under the tide." A $150k/month business may sound sexy on the surface but when shit hit the fan, she was "grinding" and starting her income over every month. She wasn't strategic.

She had no recurring income in place. She still needed "new" clients every month in her business or it wouldn't succeed. She always needs "more" strategy sessions to stay afloat. The business requires her to keep running Facebook ads to get new people.

A business that can be shut off just losing 1 source is dangerously vulnerable. The loneliest number in business is one.

- 1 Facebook ad.
- 1 offer.
- 1 webinar.
- 1 market need.
- 1 enrollment process.
- 0 recurring clients.

This type of business is 100% percent dependent on constant "new". This means she cannot escape the grind/rat race. It's built on a foundation of quicksand.

Escape The Grind Of Starting Over Each Month

After my 2008 depression, my otherworldly ayahuasca experiences gave me time to deeply think about what to do differently. Because I too was grinding and never getting ahead.

Because the best way to solve this problem is to start with getting one lifetime recurring client. One client that she can continue to help and serve. Chances are once she solved that person's problem, someone else would also want the same offer. Before long she would have a whole slew of people paying her every month *before* she ran a single Facebook ad or got on another strategy session. She would have a recurring customer base to build a real foundation on.

Remember: The first of the month should be payday instead of worry day.

You want to help both you and your clients build this real foundation. Do not get preoccupied with "new" and throw away the real asset. Value above all your relationship with your customers.

During hard times, digital marketing agencies are one of the first "expenses" to get cut. If you want to win in hard times, it's important to understand why. You must understand the deeper real reason why.

When hard times happen and clients let you go, there is a 99% chance they let you go because they have cash flow problems. It also means you can probably get them back. That's important to you. Why?

Because it's not because they don't like you, they don't like your service, or they don't see your value. It just means they had to make some difficult choices.

Bringing Back "Lost" Clients

Remember that Seinfeld episode where George tries to break up with Maura? She says "no". Baffled by it, George is forced to stay together. Be Maura. Don't break up with your clients, especially the good ones, just because times are hard.

Here's a little script you can use to get back a good client. "Hey (Name), can I ask you a question? I know cash flow is pretty tight right now. That's probably why you had to let us go. I had a new idea and to get some extra clients/patients/customers. This new strategy works in addition to what we've been doing. I've tested it small so far and it's worked for some other people. If you didn't have to pay until after it was successful, would it be possible to run a little test campaign?"

One last shameless plug. If you want this template and other ones grab yours free at beyondagencyprofits.com. There's no need for you to reinvent the wheel.

Be a source of cash flow. Even in hard times, you will be in demand. Be prepared. Build your recurring client base and assets. During the worst of times, you will succeed even more. Sources of cash flow can always write their own ticket anytime and any place. You are writing your own destiny.

Chapter 14: Beginning With The End In Mind

What is the purpose of your agency? How does it serve the bigger picture in your life? Does it work for you or are you working for it? Does it build freedom and acquire assets? Does it bring you joy, happiness, and fulfillment?

Most people settle. They run an agency that is about settling. They settle for the clients they think they can get, they take their credit card, and then they eek out a decent living providing an average service.

Just to be clear, there is absolutely nothing wrong with that. It's just a very hard way to make your living. It's not very fulfilling. It's a lot of "grinding" month after month.

It's also "damned if you do and damned if you don't". Why? Because it will create either money or time. You almost never get both together. Success will drown you in unending busyness and lack of success will make you worry about a lack of cash in the bank.

What you are creating for yourself is something altogether different. It involves your *conscious intentional decision*. It is *your decision to live on purpose*.

Choosing To Live Consciously, Intentionally, And Purposefully

It is choosing to live the life you were meant to live. It is living your reality on your terms. It is creating a meaningful difference for your clients and adding value to the world in a strategic leveraged way.

You are creating success in both money and time together. That harmonious balance always has a trickle down effect to your relationships, confidence, families, spirituality, and other aspects of your life. You are doing it in a way that provides real lasting fulfillment.

Dare To Dream A Life Worth Living

If you could snap your fingers and have your dream agency now, who would you work with? When and how often would you work? What would you do? Where would you most love to do it? What do you absolutely love about it? What kind of difference are you making in the world?

Think long and hard about your answers. Because they form the basis for what kind of agency you can have. You must first hold it inside yourself as possible. You must see it in your mind before you can see it out there. Then you can live it as your everyday life.

You deserve the best life possible. Dare to dream. Live big. Live on purpose.

May the force be with you.

About The Author

Frankie Fihn has been in digital marketing since 2007. He is a shaman, speaker, author, entrepreneur and world traveler. He has been featured with the world's number one marketer Jay Abraham. He has also written for several magazines, he has been featured in numerous podcasts and articles, and he has spoken on stages all across the world. His approach covers lifestyle design, asset creation, client selection, leverage, and spirituality. He invites readers to email him at frankie@beyondagencyprofits.com.

Printed in Great Britain
by Amazon